Legislative

DATE DUE			

Legislative Influence on Corporate Pension Plans

Dennis E. Logue

American Enterprise Institute for Public Policy Research
Washington, D.C.

Dennis E. Logue is associate professor of business administration at the Amos Tuck School of Business Administration, Dartmouth College.

Library of Congress Cataloging in Publication Data

Logue, Dennis E
  Legislative influence on corporate pension plans.

  (AEI studies ; 234)
  1. Pension trusts—United States. I. Title.
II. Series: American Enterprise Institute for
Public Policy Research. AEI studies ; 234.
KF3512.L63   344'.73'01252   79-11589
ISBN 0-8447-3337-7

AEI Studies 234

Printed in the United States of America

CONTENTS

PREFACE

For corporate pension programs difficult times lie ahead. Security markets—and hence the nominal values of pension fund assets—have not kept up with inflation, and the rate of corporate contributions has not accelerated sufficiently to close the gap. As a consequence, many corporate pension funds may now be inadequately funded. Perhaps even more significant, corporate pension policies have been subjected to intense internal reevaluation as a result of government legislative actions. This study will focus on the effects on private pensions of the Employee Retirement Income Security Act of 1974 (ERISA) and of changes in the social security system.

ERISA has tended to standardize the terms for vesting and eligibility requirements in pension fund contracts. Moreover, it has established funding standards and created a new quasi-government pension insurance agency, the Pension Benefits Guarantee Corporation. The net effect of the changes has been to reduce the benefits to employers of offering pension plans to their employees. The act also created the opportunity for employees who are not covered by private pension plans to save for retirement through their own tax-deferred savings plans, or individual retirement accounts. As a result, the special tax-related attractions of private pension plans have been reduced. All things considered, the act will unambiguously lead to a reduction in the demand for corporate pension plans.

The social security system also is creating disincentives for corporate pension plans. As expected social security benefits rise, the work incentives produced by a pension of a given dollar size tend to diminish. This in turn reduces corporate incentives to provide pensions. Similarly, as social security taxes rise, the individual's general capacity or inclination to save declines, and this tends to reduce employee demand for corporate pension programs which save on the employee's behalf. All in all, the social security system reduces the relative desirability of corporate pension programs.

Two significant legislative influences are acting in consort. Both have substantial potential for reducing the number and size of corporate pension programs at least in relation to what they might otherwise have been. Whether this is desirable or not is unknown. But the fact itself is, of course, of great interest and significance, for it implies that ultimately government will have a greater role in satisfying retirement income needs.

This study has benefited greatly from the insightful, helpful, and patient comments of Colin Campbell. I am most grateful to him. George Oldfield and Roger Murray carefully read the entire manuscript and made many useful suggestions. Robert Guest, John Hennessey, and Robert Macdonald also commented extensively on portions of the manuscript. Finally, I offer thanks to Barbara Haskell who typed many drafts of the manuscript with her customary good cheer and precision.

1
Introduction

Recent years have witnessed an explosion of concern over the administration and funding of private and public pension programs. The Employee Retirement Income Security Act of 1974 (ERISA)[1] focused attention on the way in which private industrial pension plans are set up and run. Partly as a result of this legislation and the publicity it brought to the corporate pension system, and partly because of the increasing size, coverage, and importance of private pension funds— approximately 30 million covered employees and $200 billion in assets in 1976—a heavy flow of research has been aimed at analyzing not only the financial aspects but also the managerial and social implications of the private industrial pension system.[2] Similarly, public employees' pension funds have been scrutinized.[3] Finally, the social security system itself has been subjected to many analyses, ranging from the basic philosophy of the program, through its financial soundness, to the implications for economic behavior.[4]

---

[1] Public Law 93-406, 93rd Congress, 2d session, September 2, 1974.

[2] See, for example, Jack L. Treynor, Patrick J. Regan, and William W. Priest, Jr., *The Financial Reality of Pension Funding under ERISA* (Homewood, Ill.: Dow-Jones–Irwin, 1976); William F. Sharpe, "Corporate Pension Funding Policy," *Journal of Financial Economics*, vol. 3 (June 1976), pp. 183–193; and Peter F. Drucker, *The Unseen Revolution: How Pension Fund Socialism Came to America* (New York: Harper and Row, 1976).

[3] See, for instance, Robert Tilove, *Public Employee Pension Funds*, Twentieth Century Fund Report (New York: Columbia University Press, 1976).

[4] As an example of the philosophical inquiry, see Martin S. Feldstein, "Seven Principles of Social Insurance," *Challenge* (December 1976), pp. 6–11, and "Social Insurance" in Colin D. Campbell, ed., *Income Redistribution* (Washington, D.C.: American Enterprise Institute, 1977), pp. 71–97; financial aspects are analyzed in J. W. Van Gorkom, *Social Security—The Long-Term Deficit* (Washington, D.C.: American Enterprise Institute, 1976); general economic implications are explored in Martin S. Feldstein, "Social Security, Induced Retirement, and Aggregate Capital Accumulation," *Journal of Political Economy*, vol. 82 (September/October 1974), pp. 905–926.

Wholly apart from its substance, the volume and diversity of research suggests that many critical questions regarding the overall system of pension programs and pension fund management remain unanswered. Moreover, the general tone of most inquiries conveys a sense of uneasiness about the entire pension or retirement income system. Discussion with business executives confirms this prevailing sense of uneasiness about the state of all pension systems, and of private industrial pension systems in particular.[5] In short, business and academia seem to share the view that something may be amiss with the pension system, but the substance of these concerns has yet to be identified. This is partly because there is no concise statement of what pension programs are supposed to do for firms and no systematically organized examination of pertinent data.

This study will attempt to clarify at least a portion of these more general concerns. In particular, several aspects of private industrial pension programs and their relationship to the social security system will be analyzed. The study will endeavor to uncover the source of unease on the part of the business community—the providers of private pensions—and will consider what courses firms might take. Employment and retirement benefits other than pensions, such as life insurance and health benefits, will not be treated here, although for many firms these benefits are nearly as costly as pension benefits. For the most part, such benefits have been unaffected by recent legislation.

This study will concentrate on private, industrial, defined benefit pension programs rather than on defined contribution or money purchase plans. This is not because the latter are unimportant but because most large firms have defined benefit plans. They offer retirees a fixed sum every period upon retirement, and typically the amount is a function of the number of years on the job and pay during all or part of the period of employment. Defined contribution plans are fundamentally different in that employees' claims usually vest immediately, and the principal factor determining pension benefits is how well the funds perform, not the policies pursued by the sponsoring firms. Thus the problems faced by firms offering defined benefit plans are very different from those faced by firms offering defined contribution plans.

This study analyzes primarily the benefits and costs of the private pension system to firms and their employees. It discusses investment

---

[5] At a conference on pension funds at the Amos Tuck School of Business Administration, Dartmouth College, February 27 through March 1, 1977, the general attitude of the business participants toward the private pension system was one of deep concern and uneasiness.

management of pension funds only tangentially. Further, it explores the integration that has taken place between private industrial pension plans and the social security system. The central issue is: Are private and public pension systems still worthwhile, or is their value to sponsoring firms, and employees as well, being undermined by various legislative actions? Are pension programs likely to continue as they currently exist, or will private industrial pension systems decline in importance?

The conclusion of this study is pessimistic. ERISA appears to be based on an erroneous view of the private pension program. It has raised the cost of corporate pension programs and simultaneously reduced the benefits of these programs to firms. As evidence, between the end of 1974 and July 1977 nearly 30 percent of all private pension plans were terminated.[6] Although most of these plans were small, the percentage decline is still significant.

At the same time, recent sharp increases in social security benefits have made corporate pensions less valuable. To achieve the same measure of worker incentives from their pension programs as in the past, firms would have to increase their pensions proportionately more than wages. This appears unlikely. As a consequence of ERISA and rising social security benefits (and costs), and because recent tax legislation enables employees to establish personal pension plans (individual retirement accounts) that yield the same kind of tax advantages as corporate plans, the growth of corporate pension coverage will probably decline. In addition, firms whose pension programs were marginal or nearly so will eliminate their programs entirely, and other firms will reduce the benefits provided.

Chapter 2 provides a brief résumé of the economic reasons for concern over the future of the private industrial pension system. The costs of the dual (private and public) pension system both to firms and to the nation are rising at an alarming rate not seen when the programs were initially established. This is especially true of social security.

Chapter 3 reviews and extends the theory of pensions and explains why private pensions have become such an important component of employees' total compensation packages. Though tax savings have played a considerable role, other reasons for the size and growth of pension plans relate to the organization of large firms. Pensions are contingent payment contracts, dependent upon good job performance by the employee. This was the early motivation for private pension arrangements, the first of which was that of the American Express Company in 1875. This rationale is neglected by ERISA, which pre-

---

[6] *New York Times*, September 8, 1977, section 4, p. 2.

sumes that pensions are only deferred wages, the right to which is immediately deserved by the employee.

Chapter 4 considers trends in the components of private industrial pension plans. It shows that benefit formulas have not become overly generous but that the vesting and age and eligibility requirements have been loosened substantially. The higher cost to firms of pensions is attributable to these features rather than to changes in the basic pension formulas.

Chapter 5 includes an analysis of the impact of ERISA on corporate pension policies. Although much attention has been given to its provisions for pension funding and fund administration, other mandates, principally the new vesting and eligibility requirements, have had perhaps the most important effects. Ironically, ERISA may cause widespread termination of pension plans.

Chapter 6 treats the integration of social security with private industrial pensions and examines the reason for congressional concern over private pension systems in light of changes in the social security system. Strengthening the social security system weakens the incentive for firms to offer private pensions, hence social security (without the aid of ERISA) may reduce the importance of the private pension system.

Chapter 7 summarizes the principal findings of the study and evaluates the future of the private corporate pension system.

2
Financial Aspects of the U.S. Private Pension System

Table 1 shows that in terms of number of workers covered, the magnitude of pension fund assets, and the number of beneficiaries, the private pension system has grown extremely rapidly since World War II.[1]

But the fact that private pension plans have grown rapidly in the past is no assurance that they will continue to do so; nor is it reasonable to assume that the large number of workers covered, the size of pension fund assets, or the number of beneficiaries would cause individual firms to worry about their pension systems. Rather, something of a much more direct nature must be at the root of their concern. Individual firms appear to be either experiencing or expecting a major reduction in the benefits relative to the cost of sponsoring a pension system. This chapter examines the relevant aggregate data, which show that the growth of private pension benefits has been dwarfed by growth in social security benefits. This, along with the pension contract changes mandated by ERISA, has sharply reduced the attractiveness of corporate pension plans.

Pension Benefits

One obvious concern of firms offering private pension plans could be the rising level of pension benefits. Have the benefit levels, hence the costs, simply gotten out of hand?

Figure 1 shows, in constant 1970 dollars, the average annual benefit paid by private pension plans to beneficiaries from 1950 through

---

[1] The growth of the private industrial pension system has been well documented and analyzed. See William C. Greenough and Francis P. King, *Pension Plans and Public Policy* (New York: Columbia University Press, 1976), especially chaps. 2 and 4; Norman B. Ture, *The Future of Private Pension Plans* (Washington, D.C.: American Enterprise Institute, 1976); and Alfred M. Skolnik, "Private Pension Plans, 1950–74," *Social Security Bulletin*, vol. 39 (June 1976), pp. 3–17.

5

TABLE 1

GROWTH OF PRIVATE PENSION FUNDS

(in millions)

	1974	1970	1965	1960	1955	1950
Covered employees (number)	29.8	29.7	25.3	21.2	15.4	9.8
Employer contributions[a]	23,020	12,580	7,370	4,710	3,280	1,750
Benefit payments[a]	12,930	7,360	3,520	1,720	850	370
Beneficiaries (number)	6.39	4.72	2.75	1.78	0.98	0.45
Assets (book value)[a]	191,700	137,100	86,500	52,000	27,500	12,100

[a] In constant 1970 dollars.

SOURCE: American Council of Life Insurance, *Pension Facts* (New York, 1976).

1974. Included are all private industrial pension plans, trusteed and insured, contributory and noncontributory, and defined benefit plans and defined contribution plans. Surprisingly, in real terms this amount has risen very little, from approximately $1,300 a year in 1950 to slightly more than $1,550 in 1974. The real growth rate of average pension benefits is approximately 2 percent per year, almost the same as growth in productivity. This low growth rate of average benefits suggests that even the benefits paid to the most recent groups of retirees have not risen particularly rapidly.

Because benefit payments have not become overly generous, they ought not to be a cause for alarm. Although averages mask many factors, and some individual firms may have promised more than can be realistically delivered, average benefit levels do not account for the concern over pensions. One source of uneasiness is the possibility that firms might be forced, through law, to index postretirement benefits against inflation. This would create a serious problem because the rate of return on pension fund assets has not kept pace with inflation in recent years.

Figure 2 shows that the average annual retirement benefit paid by the social security system in constant 1970 dollars rose from slightly more than $800 a year in 1950 to more than $1,700 a year in 1974. The average benefit began skyrocketing shortly after 1965 partly as a result of the Older Americans Act of 1965. An expressed objective of the act is that "the older people of our Nation are entitled to . . . an adequate income in retirement in accordance with the American stand-

FIGURE 1
AVERAGE ANNUAL PRIVATE PENSION BENEFIT

Constant 1970 dollars

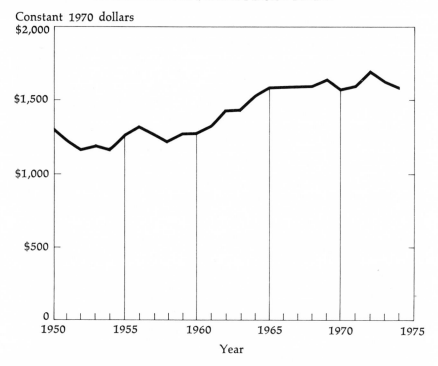

Year

SOURCE: Alfred M. Skolnik, "Private Pension Plans, 1950–74," *Social Security Bulletin*, vol. 39 (June 1976), pp. 3–17.

ard of living."[2] This contrasts sharply with the original notion that social security retirement benefits were intended to be a "floor of protection." A further sharp escalation in benefits resulted from the social security legislation of 1972.

Although many beneficiaries receive considerably less than the average, benefits have more than doubled in real terms in a quarter century. Benefits of newly retired workers have risen considerably more than the average.

Beneficiaries of a private pension are also likely to be receiving social security benefits. If this, too, is of average size, in 1974 the average retiree with a private pension received pension benefits of more than $3,200 per year in constant 1970 dollars. Relative to the national average net income in 1974 of $5,350 (in 1970 dollars), this represented

[2] Reported in Greenough and King, *Pension Plans and Public Policy*, p. xi.

FIGURE 2
AVERAGE ANNUAL SOCIAL SECURITY RETIREMENT BENEFIT

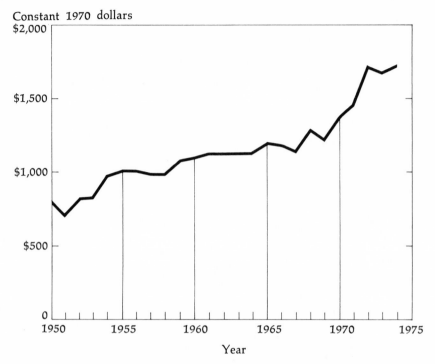

Constant 1970 dollars

Year

SOURCE: *Social Security Bulletin*, various issues.

an average replacement ratio for the wholly covered retiree of approximately 60 percent.

In the early 1950s, private pension benefits accounted for more than 61 percent of the total pension income of persons having both social security and a private pension; they now represent somewhat less than 48 percent. This shift has probably reduced the benefits to the firm of offering a private pension plan. To the extent that the objective of corporate pension plans is to strengthen work incentives and to deter labor mobility, the growth in social security must have reduced the effectiveness of corporate plans.

Pension Costs

Figure 3 shows that the annual employer contribution to private pension plans rose from slightly less than $300 per covered worker in 1950 to slightly more than $720 per covered worker in 1975 in constant

FIGURE 3
Employer Contributions Per Covered Employee

Constant 1970 dollars

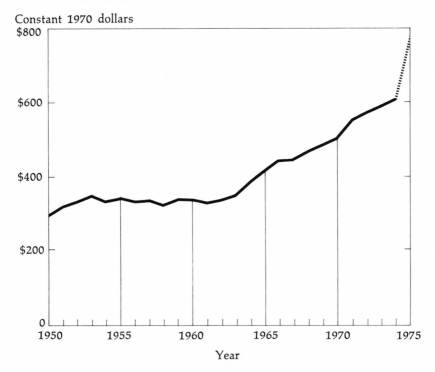

Year

Source: American Council on Life Insurance, *Pension Facts*, various issues.

dollars. In 1950, the maximum employer social security tax per employee was roughly $65.25 a year in 1970 dollars. In 1974, it was slightly more than $517.00 in 1970 dollars. Altogether, social security taxes paid by employers and private pension contributions per employee entitled to the maximum social security benefit as well as an average private pension rose from approximately $365 in 1950 to $1,237 in 1974. Including employee social security contributions brings the total to $1,754.00.

Although the cost of pension plans has risen substantially, the average benefits shown in Figure 1 have not. This is because earlier vesting and liberalization of the eligibility requirement have increased the portion of covered employees receiving pension benefits.

In view of the rapid rise in the cost of both social security and private pensions, business executives may be justified in worrying about the pension system. (These increased costs may be shifted to

TABLE 2

LEGALLY REQUIRED EMPLOYEE BENEFIT PAYMENTS AND PENSION AND OTHER BENEFIT COSTS AS A PERCENTAGE OF PAYROLL

| | Employer's share | |
Year	Legally required payments	Pension and other agreed-upon payments
1953	2.8	7.4
1955	2.9	8.3
1957	3.1	8.7
1959	3.5	9.2
1961	3.9	9.3
1963	4.5	9.5
1965	4.1	9.8
1967	4.9	10.3
1969	5.3	10.7
1971	5.5	12.4
1973	6.7	13.0

SOURCE: U.S. Chamber of Commerce, *Employee Benefits 1973* (Washington, D.C., 1974), table 19, p. 27.

employees, however, if the higher costs of such programs are offset by lower wage payments.) The large increases in social security taxes were probably unanticipated, and the total cost of financing private and social security pension benefit systems probably exceeds the cost expected by firms when private plans were originally contracted. Demographic projections that show a rising portion of the population above the age of sixty-five are a further cause of concern.[3] Firms may not be able to keep the financial promises they have made, or they will keep them only at great cost to shareholders.

Table 2 shows the legally required benefit payments (the employer's social security taxes, primarily) and pension contributions and other agreed-upon benefit payments as a percentage of total payroll for a large sample of firms. While pension and benefit payments did not quite double in importance over the 1953–1973 period, legally required payments, of which social security contributions represent nearly 80 percent, were up nearly 130 percent.[4]

[3] See those, for example, reported in James H. Schulz, *The Economics of Aging* (Belmont, Calif.: Wadsworth Publishing Co., 1976), chaps. 1 and 2. Among other data, he reports that the median age of the population will rise from 27.9 years in 1970 to 36.7 years in 2025.

[4] Data were derived from U.S. Chamber of Commerce, *Employee Benefits 1973* (Washington, D.C., 1974), pp. 8 and 27.

FIGURE 4
Ratio of Benefits Paid to Combined Employer-Employee Contributions to Private Pension Plans

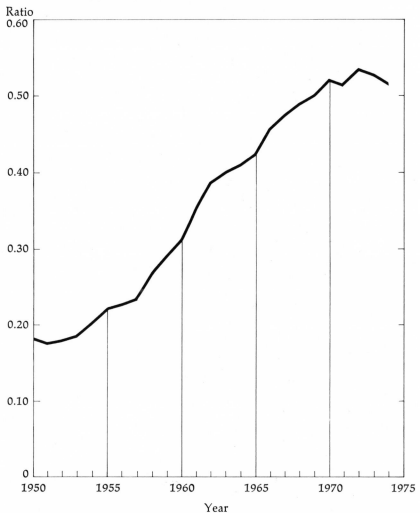

Source: Alfred M. Skolnik, "Private Pension Plans, 1950–74," *Social Security Bulletin*, vol. 39 (June 1976), pp. 3–17, table 1.

In contrast to the pay-as-you-go nature of the social security system, private industrial pension plans are typically assumed to be substantially funded, with benefits largely paid out of accumulated investment funds. The relationship between the annual amount of private pension benefits and the annual amount of combined employer-employee contributions to private pension funds is shown in Figure 4.

The ratio of benefits paid to total contributions has risen from roughly 18 percent in 1950 to more than 50 percent in 1974. Although it appears as though the private pension system has become more like a pay-as-you-go than a funded system, these data are probably misleading. As pension programs mature, steady state conditions result. If benefits paid equal 50 percent of contributions, then only 50 percent of contributions get set aside for the current work force. As the number of retired employees approximates the size of the current work force, a rise in the ratio of benefits to contributions would be expected, but without actuarial details it is hard to tell for sure.

The rise in the ratio of benefits to contributions is attributable principally to the fact that the number of retirees has increased more rapidly than the number of covered employees. This trend will probably continue. Unless firms raise their level of contributions even more rapidly in the future than they have in the past, the private pension system will probably tend toward a pay-as-you-go status, but with a large accumulated stock of pension fund assets. The system would be fully funded, but would appear to be a carousel. This could have depressing effects on the rate of new capital formation in the United States,[5] particularly if a dollar of private pension benefits leads to a decline of more than a dollar of personal discretionary saving.

ERISA requires that, in existing plans, unfunded liabilities arising from employees' past services be reduced to zero over a forty-year period; new plans or old plans with liberalized benefits must pay off unfunded liabilities in thirty years. This is a long time, but there is no guarantee that firms whose pension plans are currently underfunded will be able to provide funding this promptly. In 1975 the thirty firms with the largest unfunded vested pension liabilities (that is, the largest difference between the promised benefits already earned and the assets of their pension funds) reported these liabilities to be roughly $5 billion.[6] Treynor, Regan, and Priest have estimated that in 1975 the magnitude of unfunded vested pension benefits for all firms in the United States was between $20 billion and $60 billion.[7] These deficits

---

[5] See Alicia Munnell, "Private Pensions and Savings: New Evidence," *Journal of Political Economy*, vol. 84 (October 1976), pp. 1013–1032. Munnell demonstrates that both the social security system and the private pension system have negative effects on personal saving. The private pension system does hold primary securities, however, and hence contributes to domestic capital formation and substitutes adequately for personal savings. The social security system's primary asset is the ability to levy future taxes; it holds no primary corporate financial assets—stocks or bonds—and hence does not contribute to domestic investment.

[6] Arlene Hershman, "The Big Pension Fund Drain," *Dun's Review*, July 1975, pp. 31–35.

[7] *The Financial Reality of Pension Funding under ERISA*, p. 63, n. 6.

must be financed either externally by selling debt or equity or internally through pretax earnings, that is, amortization through earning power.

These actuarial deficits depend upon assumptions regarding future inflation and the investment performance of pension funds. If the inflation rate in the United States should accelerate and if future investment performance is as dismal as it has been during the past decade, the actual magnitude of the deficits may be much larger than they currently appear.

ERISA has forced firms to examine the cost of their pension plans. While most firms probably needed no prodding from the government to review their pension plans, some firms undoubtedly had overextended themselves. Some firms may have perceived their costs of borrowing from employees via unfunded pension benefits to be quite low and felt that returns on investment in the firm would be significantly greater than returns on pension fund assets. Similarly, some firms may have believed that their pension fund managers could achieve above average investment results.

3

A Theory of Pensions

This chapter reviews the institutionalist explanation of the growth of private pension plans and two theories of private pensions—one suggesting that pensions are altruistic rewards for years of service, the other suggesting that pensions are nothing more than deferred wages. There are wide disparities, however, between both these descriptions and the pension fund practices that are commonly observed. An alternative theory is therefore presented, based on recent developments in the theory of organizational behavior, particularly agency relationships, and in capital market theory. If it is assumed that private pensions are contingent claims on the firm (a type of "call option"), and that payment is conditional on the satisfactory completion of certain employment obligations, observable pension practices can be explained quite well. This theory also helps explain why defined benefit plans benefit owners more than defined contribution plans do. It describes the financial arrangements of pension funds and makes clear why firm's creditors (bondholders) might prefer large unfunded pension liabilities despite their lack of any obvious advantage over small or zero unfunded liabilities.

Attention is focused on defined benefit plans, the most common type of industrial pension plan. These have a fixed benefit that is virtually independent of the performance of pension fund assets and are, at least nominally, all or partly funded by employer contributions.

An Institutionalist View of Pension Growth

Though private pension plans have existed since 1875 when the American Express Company inaugurated its plan,[1] they covered only

---

[1] For an interesting review of the history of private pension plans see Greenough and King, *Pension Plans and Public Policy*, chap. 2.

about 3 or 4 million workers before 1935.[2] Only railroads, a few industrial companies, the federal government, and state and local governments had plans prior to 1940. The industrial plans typically involved no more than the purchase of a life insurance company annuity and were unfunded before the employee's retirement or disablement. Pension benefits were almost always at the discretion of the firm and were seldom contractual obligations.

In the late 1940s and in the 1950s, there was a surge in the growth of private industrial pension programs that made the earlier experience, especially the highly discretionary payment policies, seem unusual. Some analysts attributed the existence of early private pension plans to ad hoc factors and concluded that the private industrial pension system grew principally as a result of some peculiar features of the financial markets and the national scene. The following factors were frequently cited:[3]

- The passage of the Social Security Act of 1935 and the Social Security Amendments of 1939 heightened awareness of the financial problems of old age and elicited a demand for private pension plans.

- The Revenue Act of 1921 coupled with the Internal Revenue Act of 1942 made private pensions attractive for tax reasons. The 1942 act made pension contributions by employers tax deductible, exempted income on the pension plans from taxation and exempted employees from taxation of that portion of income contributed to pension funds, and deferred taxation of pension fund income until it was paid out in the form of retirement benefits. At that time, presumably, the wage earner's tax bracket would be lower than during work years.

- Wage stabilization programs during World War II and the Korean War prevented firms from giving direct pay increases and induced firms to give hidden wage increases in the form of pension benefits.

- Court decisions in 1948 to 1950 made pension benefits a legitimate collective bargaining issue as defined under the Labor Management Relations Act of 1947.

- Labor unions, discontented with the magnitude of social security

---

[2] Schulz, *Economics of Aging*, p. 113.

[3] These are reported in Paul P. Harbrecht, *Pension Funds and Economic Power* (New York: Twentieth Century Fund, 1959), chap. 1. Original references include, most notably, U.S. Securities and Exchange Commission, *Survey of Corporate Pension Funds, 1951–1954* (Washington, D.C., 1956).

benefits, directed their efforts away from seeking expanded government solutions and toward obtaining retirement benefits from private employers.

- Increasing life expectancy made it difficult to rely upon natural mechanisms for eliminating older, less productive employees and created a need for financial inducements to retire.

- It was commonly believed that the costs of investing and managing large corporate pension funds were lower than the costs to individual investors and that funds could be expected to grow more quickly under professional management.

- The expanded investment opportunities available to pension funds rather than to individuals induced firms to set up pension programs.

Each of these factors probably contributed to the growth of private pension plans, but concentration on these historical developments directs attention away from the more fundamental economic forces also at work. During this period, the structure of business organizations was changing. As firms became larger, decision making became decentralized and ways were sought to control the decisions made by semi-autonomous agents. Further, as financing arrangements became more complex, ownership of firms became more diffuse, and increased attention had to be paid to what the non-share-owning (or relatively small shareholder) managers were doing. The earliest pension plans were established by relatively large, geographically dispersed firms with widespread ownership. Pension plans helped in the management of these firms, particularly the monitoring and control of employee behavior.

Predictions made from the institutional perspective are different from those made on the basis of economic analysis. This does not imply that such institutional factors are unimportant, but that economic analysis may also be useful and may give better predictions of future developments. A purely institutionalist view might very well lead to the conclusion that ERISA and the recent expansion of social security benefits will have only marginal effects on the private pension system, but, as will be argued below, economic analysis suggests that the impact of these changes will be profound.

Pensions as Altruism

In the early 1900s, perceptions about the private industrial pension system in the United States emphasized that firms had a "social

16

responsibility" to provide older workers with adequate retirement income. One expert, writing in 1912, argued that "From the standpoint of the whole system of social economy no employer has a right to engage men in any occupation that exhausts the individual's industrial life in 10, 20, or 40 years; and then leave the remnant floating on society at large as a derelict at sea."[4]

The concept of "human depreciation" was widely held in the late 1940s and, indeed, was espoused by such disparate groups as the Steel Industry Board in 1949 and the United Auto Workers–Confederation of Industrial Organizations.[5] In fact, in nearly all pension plans negotiated by the UAW-CIO (prior to the CIO's merger with the American Federation of Labor [AFL] and the separation of the UAW) pension benefits were determined on the basis of a specified dollar amount multiplied by years of service, and little regard was paid to workers' actual earnings. The type of benefit adopted was based on the concept of human depreciation, and pensions were also considered a reward for loyalty.

In the early private pension systems, workers usually had no contractual right to pensions, despite (often ambiguous) employer promises to the contrary. One typical form of company disclaimer in some plans was:

> This pension plan is a voluntary act on the part of the company and is not to be deemed or construed to be a part of any contract of employment, or as giving any employee an enforceable right against the company. The board of directors of the company reserves the right to alter, amend, or annul or cancel the plan or any part of it at any time. The right of the company to discharge any employee at any time shall not be affected by this plan, nor shall such employee have any interest in any pension after discharge.[6]

Indeed, employer behavior consistent with the wording of this disclaimer was upheld in several court decisions.[7] Plans could be termi-

---

[4] Lee Welling Squires, *Old Age Dependency in the United States* (New York: Macmillan, 1912), p. 272, cited in Harbrecht, *Pension Funds and Economic Power*, p. 74.

[5] Steel Industry Board, *Report to the President of the United States on the Labor Dispute in the Basic Steel Industry*, September 10, 1949, p. 11.

[6] Cornelius Justin and Mario Impellizeri, "The Mirage of Private Pensions," *Private Welfare and Pension Plan Legislation*, Hearings before General Subcommittee on Labor, House Committee on Education and Labor, 91st Congress, 1st and 2nd sessions (Washington, D.C., 1970), p. 388; cited in Robert Taggart, "The Labor Market Impacts of the Private Pension System," in Subcommittee on Fiscal Policy of the Joint Economic Committee, 93rd Congress, 1st session, Studies in Public Welfare, Paper no. 11 (Washington, D.C., 1973), p. 41.

[7] McNevin v. Solvay Process Co., 32 Appl. Div., New York (1898); and Dolge v. Dolge, 75 New York Suppl. (1902).

nated arbitrarily and long-time employees dismissed with no pension benefits, even when the employer had gone so far as to issue passbooks indicating how much money had been "set aside" for employees as of particular dates.

As this example shows, both management and labor viewed pensions as gratuities provided by enlightened employers, who believed that employees, like machines, not only depreciate but also are improvident and must be cared for financially in their old age. The only difference between the attitudes of labor and management was that organized labor viewed pensions as rights to be bargained and contracted for and management expressed a preference for allotting them on a discretionary basis.

The Deferred Wage Theory of Pensions

Since the late 1940s, the altruistic view has gradually been replaced by the concept of pensions as deferred wages. The Inland Steel Decision in 1947 was a benchmark in bringing about the change; at that time, the National Labor Relations Board ruled:

> Realistically viewed, this type of wage enhancement or increase [pensions], no less than any other, becomes an integral part of the entire wage structure, and the character of the employee representative's interest in it and the terms of its grants is no different than any other case where a change in the wage is affected.[8]

The AFL adopted a similar position:

> It [the deferred wage theory] means, first that the worker's interest in the pension fund is not established solely by reason of advanced age and "long and faithful" service with an employer. That interest is established by reason of the work performed by all members during the term of the contract.[9]

The deferred wage approach to pensions implies that the employee's total compensation tends to equal his marginal product. The marginal product is then split into instantaneous compensation—such as wages and immediately realizable fringe benefits—and pension claims. It further implies that the primary determinants of the split are the value of the income tax deferral and the difference between the

---

[8] Taggart, "Labor Market Impacts of the Private Pension System," p. 41.

[9] American Federation of Labor, *Pension Plans under Collective Bargaining: A Reference Guide for Trade Unions* (no date), p. v, cited in Harbrecht, *Pension Funds and Economic Power*, pp. 95, 96.

rate of return employees could achieve individually by investing the money they would otherwise receive as wages, and what employers could achieve by actively managing the pension funds, either by investing in a diversified market portfolio or by retaining the funds in the business. Although a pay-as-you-go approach to pension funding would result if funds were retained in the business, the pension fund would still be backed by real assets.

There are strong grounds for the belief that pensions are nothing more than deferred wages. In plans with defined contributions and where accruals vest immediately, the pension is a deferred wage designed to take advantage of tax laws, more attractive investment opportunities, or less costly investment transactions. If employees anticipate being in a lower income tax bracket after retirement and if expected returns on pension fund contributions managed by firms are not less than the returns achievable by individuals, employees would always be better off with a portion of their wages going to pension funds. This assumes that employees could borrow against their pension fund claims if funds were needed to supplement current income. Moreover, in a competitive labor market a worker would not accept employment if the compensation "portfolio" offered had less value to him than some other available elsewhere.

Though the deferred wage concept of pensions is applicable to some pension plans, it does not apply to the most common types. Most pension payments contain not only a deferred wage component based on the employee's marginal product, but also incentive features such as delayed vestings and defined benefits. In addition, many private pension plans are integrated with social security.

Vesting. Most private pension plans in the United States do not vest immediately. Normally, a contractual pension claim exists only after the employee has worked for an employer for a specified number of years. Also, pension contracts typically specify that age and experience requirements must be filled before the employee is eligible for a pension. Recent legislation has liberalized, but not eliminated, these requirements.

Under typical eligibility and vesting provisions, some employees will never receive a pension from a particular employer.[10] Although there must be a compelling incentive for an employee to relinquish a claim to current earnings in return for a less than unitary probability

---

[10] See Greenough and King, *Pension Plans and Public Policy*, chap. 7; Taggart, "Labor Market Impacts of the Private Pension System," chaps. 3 and 4 and references cited therein.

of receiving them, plus interest, in the future, such compelling incentives are not obvious. It is often argued that astute pension fund management by employers yields returns considerably larger than those that employees could earn if they held the assets individually. Even if the funds were paid out in a form allowing employees to take advantage of the income tax deferral,[11] employers could still afford to pay pension benefits in excess of those that employees could generate through personal investment. But there is no reason for employers to pay more if pension benefits are only deferred wages. And if pension payments are not greater than the future value of deferred wages, there is no reason for employees to bear the risk introduced by vesting and eligibility requirements.

Defined Benefit Plans. Most industrial pension plans are defined benefit plans rather than defined contribution plans, and the firm assumes the financial risks associated with the pension fund rather than shifting them to the employee.

Defined benefit arrangements are inexplicable under the deferred wage theory of pensions. Under such arrangements, pension payments are generally fixed by a formula that takes account of years of service and earnings, but not the actual realized return on the pension fund assets. The employer has no obvious incentive to bear the risk that the financial return on the pension fund's assets will not meet actuarial expectations. Of course, the firm managers can employ these funds as they would any other, but why is setting up a pension fund a better use than others? If employers assume that the employee would not obtain a financial return much different from that achieved by the employer, then defined benefit plans could be eliminated in favor of defined contribution plans.[12] In reality, *employer* compensation for

---

[11] Since 1976 the law allows employees not covered by private pension plans to establish individual retirement accounts (IRAs) for up to 15 percent or $1,500 (whichever is lower) of their earnings annually without paying income tax on that portion. Such a tax break would probably not have been enacted if private industrial pension plans had not expanded their coverage as rapidly as they did. The tax advantages for individual retirement savings were probably enacted because of a perceived inequity between employees who were covered by private pension plans and those who were not, including the self-employed.

[12] This view is slightly different from that in Treynor, Regan, and Priest, *Financial Reality of Pension Funding under ERISA*, chaps. 1, 3, and 4. According to the authors, pension fund risks are borne mostly by the beneficiaries, while the rewards from superior portfolio performance accrue to the sponsoring company.

This view would be correct if pensions were merely deferred wages. But it offers no explanation of why employees would allow themselves to lose, through no direct fault of their own, income for which they had already worked. Because employees accept such conditions, it must be assumed either that they are irrational

risk bearing derives from the vesting provisions and eligibility requirements of private pension plans. The employee, in return, is compensated for bearing the risk of not meeting vesting requirements by a reduction in the variability of investment return—the firm buffers the employee from the vagaries of security market returns. The deferred wage view does not allow these trade-offs.

Integration. In many pension plans the benefit paid by the firm varies inversely with the retired employee's social security benefits. If private pensions were only deferred wages, this would be unfair. Integration of social security and private plans is an *ex post* type of adjustment. The unfairness arises because a promised pension can be reduced as a result of changes in social security benefits unrelated to past contributions. If social security is viewed as an intergenerational transfer and pensions are considered to be deferred wages, the firm should not integrate its pension system. If pensions are merely deferred wages, firms would have no right to take away from the employee deferred wages the employee has legitimately earned. Similarly, why would employees allow firms to do this, given the relative competitiveness of domestic labor markets? This general issue is discussed in Chapter 6, but the question of fairness to employees is raised here to undermine the deferred wage theory.

Other Problems. Two additional problems relate to the deferred wage theory of pensions. First, many plans routinely grant postretirement increases in pension benefits, although this would be unnecessary if pensions were merely deferred wages. Benefits may be increased, however, as an incentive to future generations of workers. Second, not all employees in private industry are covered by private pensions or other retirement plans. Such plans are generally not costly to run,

---

or that the deferred wage theory is incomplete. If the latter assumption is correct, it follows (and will be argued later) that employers (that is, shareholders) bear the risk of pension fund performance in defined benefit plans but derive compensation for this risk from vesting provisions and eligibility requirements. The mischaracterization by Treynor, Regan, and Priest stems from their acceptance of the deferred wage notion.

This view also assumes that firms with unsuccessful pension fund investment management tend to renege on their contracts. This is generally not true, especially for large firms. The frequency with which the Studebaker Corporation case of the early 1960s is cited is evidence of the rarity of similar cases, and to offer this as proof of reneging is tantamount to arguing that most automobiles are commercial failures by pointing to the Edsel. Moreover, at the time of its last pension contract, Studebaker was not particularly creditworthy. It was in no position to offer a "defined benefit" plan, and it would be hard, in my judgment, to argue that the employees did not sense this.

and if their advantages are attributable solely to tax deferrals and investment fund management, there is no reason significantly more employers do not offer them and substantially more workers do not insist on them. The fact that many employers and employees do not participate in private pension programs does not square well with the deferred wage theory.

Impact of Deferred Wage Theory

Despite conceptual difficulties with the deferred wage theory of pensions, many analysts and public policy advocates have accepted this view and have urged the development and adoption of public policies that embody it.[13] They urge earlier vesting of pension benefits, eased eligibility requirements, improved portability (that is, the ability of workers to take pension benefits with them when changing jobs from one firm to another, thus enhancing labor mobility), and different ways of funding pension plans. Many of these changes are included in ERISA.[14] If pension benefits were only deferred wages, these recommendations would not be necessary because they would already be part of private employment contracts. That is, if they simply ratify rights that employees should have, then a relatively efficient labor market would have introduced them without legislation. Only if employers behave monopsonistically in the labor market can one explain why pension arrangements seem systematically to exploit employees under the deferred wage theory. There is little evidence, however, that employers exploit employees. If employers were monopsonistic, there would be no incentive to pay pensions at all.

The basic error embodied in the recent legislation stems from the fact that private pensions are not simply deferred wages. Although they are considered deferred income for tax purposes, they have a different and important role in the employment relation—that of providing incentives to employees. This role explains the current practices of the private industrial pension system and the relationship of the private system to social security. In light of this role of pensions in the employment relation, the recent changes in legislation and in social security may weaken rather than strengthen the industrial pension system.

---

[13] See, for example, Morton C. Bernstein, *The Future of Private Pensions* (New York: Free Press, 1964), and Greenough and King, *Pension Plans and Public Policy*, chaps. 7 and 8.

[14] These changes will be discussed in some detail in Chapter 5.

Pensions as Contingent Claims

Most defined benefit pension programs have the same characteristics.[15] First, in most plans, to acquire a legal claim on pension fund assets and qualify for pension payments, an employee must work for the firm for a specified number of years.[16] Second, employees do not automatically become eligible for pension plan participation but must satisfy specified age and service requirements. Third, pension payments typically vary with salary, and in recent years firms have tended to depend not upon the entire salary history of the employee, but on the salary over the three to five years prior to retirement. Fourth, many pension funds are not fully funded, that is, the present value of pension liabilities exceeds the present value of assets.[17] Employees who otherwise qualify for vested pension benefits may not collect the full amount due them even under the pension guarantees required by ERISA because the maximum payment guaranteed is currently $750 per month. This guaranteed amount will vary with changes in the social security wage base.

Because of these characteristics of private pension plans, an employee bears a considerable amount of risk. At the time an employee is hired, he or she accepts a contingent claim against the firm, a "call option."[18] The net value of the claim is zero if the employee quits or is fired prior to vesting. Once vested, the value rises according to an agreed-upon formula.

Explicit recognition of the pension claim as a contingent contract allows a more precise contrast between the altruistic and deferred wage theories of pensions. The pension as gratuity has no contract implica-

---

[15] Data supporting these assertions will be presented in Chapters 4 and 5.

[16] There is some evidence that many employees who work for private firms offering pension plans never actually qualify for pension benefits. See Ralph Nader and Kate Blackwell, *You and Your Pension* (New York: Grossman Publishers, 1973).

[17] Treynor, Regan, and Priest, *Financial Reality of Pension Funding under ERISA*, p. 63, estimated the aggregate value of unfunded vested benefits for private industrial pension funds to be on the order of $20 billion to $60 billion in 1975. This amount represents between 9 percent and 36 percent of total pension fund assets.

[18] For an elegant treatment of the valuation of contingent claims or call options, see Fischer Black and Myron Scholes, "The Pricing of Options and Corporate Liabilities," *Journal of Political Economy*, vol. 81 (May/June 1973), pp. 637–654. For the present purposes, such detail is not necessary, but one could use a set-up analogous to that of Black and Scholes to derive explicit valuation formulas. For an analysis of different types of employment contrasts, see Oliver E. Williamson, *Markets and Hierarchies: Analysis and Antitrust Implications* (New York: Free Press, 1975), chap. 4, "Understanding the Employment Relation." Though he develops the concept of a contingent claims contract, the implications for pensions are not pursued.

FIGURE 5

Value of a Pension Claim

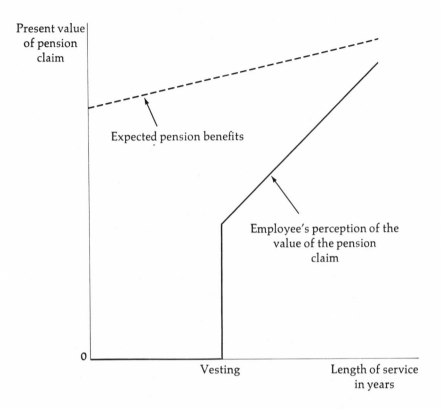

Present value of pension claim

Expected pension benefits

Employee's perception of the value of the pension claim

0

Vesting

Length of service in years

tions. The pension as pure deferred wage has a 100 percent certain contract implication; it is a right. To alter the degree of "right," one need only alter the obligations and requirements placed upon the employee. The view of pensions as a contingent claim lies between the polar extremes of the gratuity and deferred wage views.

Figure 5 illustrates the employee's perception of the value of the pension claim in relation to the fulfillment of employment obligations or term of employment. For simplicity, only the vesting provisions are considered, but other provisions could be treated similarly. The vertical axis represents the net present value of pension benefits to the employee. The horizontal axis represents the employee's length of service. Until vested, the value to the employee is zero or, in consideration of the likelihood of vesting, perhaps close to zero, as shown by the solid line. The dotted line shows the present value of expected pension benefits discounted at a risk-free rate. It assumes a career of normal length, which accounts for the high initial value. In an alternative representation, not shown, the prospective recipient might adjust the expected net present value upward annually even before vesting as the prospects for continued employment with this firm improve. In either case, however, the value rises sharply upon vesting and then typically proceeds to rise more gradually since most pension formulas pay off in relation to years of service and salary level.

If pensions were simply deferred wages, employees would insist on compensation—*in addition* to the deferred wage component of the pension—to offset the risk implied by the vesting provisions. Firms therefore must offer something more than a deferred wage.[19] They may do this through benefit sharing among employees and with the firm.

Benefit Sharing among Employees. In every group of employees hired, some will quit or be fired prior to vesting. The "deferred wages" of the departing group will not be paid to them and can be spread among the survivors. In this way, the surviving group of employees can be given claims to more than they would otherwise be entitled. From the point of view of a newly hired employee, however, the expected value of the potentially larger claim would be precisely the same as the expected value of the pension claim with immediate vesting, because of the uncertainty of being fired or leaving voluntarily.

Theory and empirical studies suggest that individuals tend to be risk averse in their financial decisions.[20] If employees view pension fund claims as financial assets, they would not view the expected value of the pension with immediate vesting as equal to that with vesting after a period of time, even though the two values may be the same. Thus, sharing the forgone deferred wages of those who leave the firm may not be enough for employees to accept the risk inherent in a contingent claim contract.

Benefit Sharing with the Firm. The second way in which firms may make the contingent claim contract attractive is by sharing with their employees some of the savings directly attributable to the contractual arrangements. Vesting provisions and other requirements for eligibil-

---

[19] Evidence provided by Munnell, "Private Pensions and Savings: New Evidence," provides some support for this conclusion. She shows (p. 1031) that firms set aside more for their employees than employees would have set aside themselves if there were no pension plan.

[20] See, for instance, Irwin Friend and Marshall Blume, "The Demand for Risky Assets," *American Economic Review*, vol. 65 (December 1975), pp. 900–922.

ity reduce labor turnover, as Schiller and Weiss show.[21] Similarly, by providing additional incentives for employees to avoid getting fired or laid off prior to vesting, such contracts induce workers to work harder with less supervision.

A lower rate of labor turnover reduces the firm's expenditures on hiring and training new employees. In addition, if workers have a financial incentive to avoid behavior that would lead to being fired and hence to losing the contingent claim, the firm can spend less on monitoring and supervising its employees. Such "savings" on expenditures for hiring, training, and supervisory functions could be passed along to employees in the form of higher compensation to offset the risk involved in taking part of their compensation in the form of an option.

In principle, this is a testable hypothesis. It suggests that the larger the hiring, training, and other costs in a particular type of employment, the more stringent should be the vesting requirement and the more generous the pension benefit schedule. There should also be a trade-off between vesting requirements and benefit levels alone, other things being equal. Unfortunately, data on hiring, training, and other costs are not usually available. Casual observation, however, reveals that in industries with relatively low training and hiring costs, such as retailing and food service, many firms do not offer pension benefits to hourly employees.

Income taxes have played and will continue to play a role in motivating pensions, because income currently paid into a qualified pension plan escapes taxation until it is withdrawn in retirement years. In the past, an individual could expect to be in a lower tax bracket after retirement, so that total taxes paid would be lower than otherwise.

Inflation has damaged this argument. As nominal incomes rise but tax rates remain unchanged, there is a distinct possibility that an individual's real tax burden in retirement will be the same as or possibly higher than in working years. Even if his or her real tax bracket is nearly the same, however, the individual who contributes to a pension plan obtains, in effect, an interest-free loan from the government. The deferment of tax payments is valuable because of the time value of money. Even if the total dollar amount of taxes that must be paid over an individual's lifetime is unaffected by pension arrangements, the present value of tax payments will be lower for the pension plan participant.

In general, the combination of incentive effects and income tax advantages motivates the establishment of private pension plans.

---

[21] Bradley R. Schiller and Randall D. Weiss, "The Impact of Private Pensions on Firm Attachment," mimeographed, 1976.

Financing the Pension Plan: An Application of the Contingent Claim Theory

The contingent claim theory depicts pensions as incentives. It explains why employees bear the risk of failure to vest and why employers might be willing to pay something extra to motivate employees to stay and to work with less supervision. To be complete, however, this theory must explain how rewards and risks are divided between employers and employees. Moreover, an analysis of the way in which pensions are financed may give further insight into and substantiation of the basic theory.

Reward Sharing. The sharing of the savings of the firm may take various forms. In defined contribution plans, the sharing could take the form of more generous pension contributions. In defined benefit plans, it could make possible more generous pension *payment* formulas. In this case, the firm would bear the risk of fluctuations in the value of the pension fund portfolio. The pension fund, in effect, holds an option against the firm to make up deficiencies in the size of the pension fund. But the firm controls, to some extent, the maturity structure of that claim through its hiring and firing practices. To maintain a long maturity structure, the firm must retain a large number of vested employees who are not near retirement age. A complex trade-off must be made between firing costs, including the pay-off on the pension claim to a fired but vested employee, and the opportunity cost of keeping that employee.

In defined benefit plans, if the realized financial returns on pension fund assets exceed expected returns, the firm benefits because it is obligated to pay only a specific amount of pension benefits; as a result of superior investment performance, the firm may reduce the level of its future contributions to the fund.[22] Benefit levels may therefore reflect, in addition to pure deferred wages, compensation to employees for risk taking in the contingent claim employment contract, and the magnitude of pension benefits will be related to "saved" expenses of hiring, training, and supervision.

Risk Sharing. The members of a typical pension plan risk not being employed long enough to receive pension benefits and also bear the risk that the firm will not be able to pay the pension benefits promised. In most cases, the firm will make up any deficits from its cash flows,

---

[22] The occurrences that prompted ERISA and the effects of that legislation modify this discussion somewhat, as discussed in Chapter 5.

but prior to ERISA firms had no legal obligation to make up such liabilities. A firm with a large pension plan deficit could voluntarily terminate the plan. In point of fact, few firms have done so, but many firms do maintain large contingent liabilities to their pension funds. These are accounted for as either unfunded vested liabilities or unfunded past service obligations, or sometimes both.[23] An unfunded obligation of the firm to the pension plan is tantamount to the pension fund's holding a risky debt claim against the firm; it is equivalent to an additional amount of "regular" debt outstanding. In effect, before ERISA the firm held a "put" option against the fund.

Ownership Interest in the Firm. Prior to ERISA, a firm could fund its plan either by issuing regular debt or equity (including transfers from retained earnings) and using the proceeds to fund the pension plan, or it could issue the debt obligation to the pension fund directly by leaving the pension plan or a portion thereof unfunded. Other things being equal, the total market value of the firm would be unaffected by whether the pension is funded through the issuance of regular debt or the issuance of corporate debt to the pension fund in the form of an unfunded corporate liability.[24]

Only recently have financial reporting requirements made it necessary for firms to report their unfunded pension liabilities. In the 1950s and early 1960s, during the rapid growth of pension plans, data on unfunded liabilities were generally not obtainable by outside analysts and investors. This sort of "off-balance sheet" financing may have increased the total market value of a firm. Investors may have been unable to detect unfunded pension liabilities, representing bond futures given to employees, or they may have considered such liabilities irrelevant because of the firm's ability to recontract pension obligations with the pension fund and thus with its employees. If the implicit interest rate on this debt were less than the growth rate of the firm, the firm would be financing at less than true market rates, and shareholders

---

[23] An unfunded vested liability is the amount by which the present value of pension fund benefits—to which employees already possess a right—exceeds the present value of pension fund assets. An unfunded past service liability or obligation occurs with a change in pension plans and is the amount by which the pension fund must be increased to provide benefits at a higher rate than under the previous agreement. See Treynor, Regan, and Priest, *Financial Reality of Pension Funding under ERISA*, chaps. 3, 4, and 5, for an excellent analysis of these issues. Among other things, they argue for using a Black-Scholes type of approach to the valuation of these pension fund claims against the firm.

[24] For a careful analysis of this proposition, see Sharpe, "Corporate Pension Funding Policy." Empirical support is found in George S. Oldfield, "Financial Aspects of the Private Pension System," *Journal of Money, Credit and Banking*, vol. 9 (February 1977), pp. 48–54.

would benefit by the issuance of this sort of debt perhaps more than by the issuance of regular debt.[25] The difference between true rates and actual rates could be split between shareowners and the pension fund. Recent changes in accounting rules tend to facilitate detection, and ERISA has virtually eliminated the ability of the firm to recontract pension promises.

Though the total market value of the firm may remain unchanged, under current accounting requirements and ERISA the relative value of debt and equity may change dramatically, depending on funding policy. In theory and practice, it is possible for equity owners of a firm to favor simultaneously increasing the risk to the debt holders and bringing potential benefits to the equity holders.[26] Consider a firm which has contractual interest payments of $40 per year and two mutually exclusive investment opportunities yielding, respectively, $40 per year with certainty and either $100 per year or, say, $39 per year with a probability of 0.5. If the first investment is made, the bondholders will receive interest payments for sure and the equity holders nothing. If the second alternative is chosen, there is a 0.5 probability that the firm will default and a 0.5 probability that equity holders will get $60.00. The bondholders would thus prefer the first, but under either set of conditions the stockholders would prefer the second. With the first investment, they receive nothing, but with the second the probability of nothing is only 0.5.

Consider another case where the firm has an unfunded obligation due the firm's pension fund. The managers and employees of the firm have a stake in the welfare of the bondholders, for they, too, hold bonds through their claims in the pension fund. Prior to ERISA, their claims were subordinate to those of most other creditors. As a result, the manager had substantially less incentive to reallocate wealth from the debt holders to the stockholders.[27]

Just as pension funds provide incentives for employees, the method in which they were typically financed benefited the bond-

[25] See Earl A. Thompson, "Debt Instruments in Both Macroeconomic Theory and Capital Theory," American Economic Review, vol. 57 (December 1967), pp. 1196–1210, for an elaboration of the logic supporting this idea.

[26] See Dan Galai and Ronald W. Masulis, "The Option Pricing Model and the Risk Factor of Stock," Journal of Financial Economics, vol. 3 (January 1976), pp. 53–81, for robust analysis and examples of this process.

[27] See Michael C. Jensen and William H. Meckling, "Theory of the Firm: Managerial Behavior, Agency Costs, and Ownership Structure," Journal of Financial Economics, vol. 3 (October 1976), pp. 305–360. They argue that the use of "inside debt" is an inexpensive way to eliminate the agency cost of the other debt holders' assuring themselves that the reallocation of wealth to shareholders is not taking place.

holders and shareholders of the firm. Because of these arrangements, funds spent on the monitoring of employees by managers, and of managers by security holders, were less than they would have been. The contingent claim theory of pensions works with respect to the financing aspects of firms as well as with their personnel practices.

The solvency of a pension fund, if there are large unfunded obligations, depends on not taking risks which unduly favor shareholders over bondholders. Similarly, the long-run viability of a firm depends on avoiding bankruptcy or default. The presence of unfunded obligations will, therefore, tend to affect the behavior of the managers who, like all other employees, have a stake in the pension fund. They will want to avoid risks which place bondholders at a particularly large disadvantage or which may have serious employment consequences (that is, job loss) for themselves. Unfunded obligations promote decision making aimed at keeping the firm in operation. In the extreme, this suggests that liabilities act to reduce the cost of monitoring employees and even management and to encourage greater employee effort. Accordingly, unfunded liabilities have much the same general effect as the call option on pensions that is a result of vesting requirements. This effect may be more important in influencing managerial behavior than in influencing the behavior of individual, nonmanagerial employees. Despite this, managers and employees would not have an incentive to ignore shareholder interests in favor of bondholders. To the extent that employees' future salaries are positively correlated with returns on the firm's equity, employees, particularly managers, have incentives to *balance* the interests of shareholders and bondholders. The existence of unfunded liabilities and the relationship of salaries to profitability should tend to motivate decision making which favors neither class of investors.

Prior to ERISA, firms with the greatest amount of unfunded pension obligations should have tended to have the greatest amount of "regular" debt. A positive relationship between the two types of debt would have been expected because there was less risk to regular debt holders of management decisions which favored equity holders. Before the recent legislation reordered the priority structure of debt claims and gave pension claims the same status as federal tax liens, unfunded pension obligations were junior to "regular" debt. Regular creditors could rely on managerial incentives to meet their claims on the earnings of the firm, because the unfunded pension liability in which the managers had a stake could not be satisfied until those claims were met. The change in priority structure has consequences for the financial valuation of the firm; it influences the magnitude of market debt that can be issued at given prices because it affects the willingness of investors to hold debt without demanding higher interest rates or more stringent debt covenants.[28] Moreover, this reordering may affect the level of pension benefits that can be promised in the future.

Incentive Effects, ERISA, and Social Security

ERISA does not recognize these incentive effects; its reform proposals are built upon the assumption that pensions are simply deferred wages. Specifics of the act will be examined later, but the main conclusion is that some provisions of ERISA will reduce the ability of firms to use pensions as incentives. This could lead to a gradual erosion of pension benefits so that pensions do ultimately become little more than deferred wages. Business should be concerned by this development because the power of an important management tool will have been stripped away.

The incentive effects of private pensions are further weakened by the increased generosity of the social security program. Two factors are at work. The first is that, as social security benefits rise, employees' needs for income from private pension plans decline. If individuals have a declining marginal rate of substitution of income for leisure, then pension plan benefits, coming as they do on top of rising social security payments, will decline in utility. The second factor is that social security tax rates are rising, and the timing of these increases has probably been unanticipated. Given these unanticipated expenses and the general difficulty of reducing real wage rates, labor costs may rise too quickly to levels that are inconsistent with full employment. The effect may be broad reductions in pensions (in lieu of reduced wages) or reductions in new hiring. If social security taxes are perfect substitutes for wages, fewer workers will be hired as social security taxes rise.[29] This issue is discussed further in Chapter 6.

---

[28] The basis for this argument may be found in Fischer Black and John C. Cox, "Valuing Corporate Securities: Some Effects of Bond Indenture Provisions," *Journal of Finance*, vol. 31 (May 1976), pp. 351–367.

[29] John A. Brittain, "The Incidence of Social Security Payroll Taxes," *American Economic Review*, vol. 61 (March 1971), pp. 110–125, has shown that there is a perfect (100 percent) trade-off between employers' social security contributions and wages paid in the intermediate and long run.

4

Trends in Corporate Pension Plans

This chapter summarizes recent trends in private industrial pension plans so as to provide a background for evaluating the impact of ERISA, the expansion of the social security system, and the development of other tax-free forms of saving for retirement.

The *Survey of Industrial Retirement Plans* published since World War II by the Bankers' Trust Company is an important source of data on pension contracts. The surveys cover approximately 180 firms employing more than 25 percent of all covered workers. Although the coverage of firms varies, substitutions of firms from period to period have been kept to a minimum, and the changes in coverage do not seriously bias the results. Even though the data are not perfectly comparable, the definitions and computation techniques have not changed so much that they would prevent identification of important trends. The data summarized are from the 1956, 1960, 1965, 1970, and 1975 surveys. The surveys made before 1956 are not used because during World War II and the Korean War and periods of price control many pension plans were being initiated or altered substantially.

The principal features of private pension contracts are: disability, death, and survivor benefits; age, service, and early retirement provisions; vesting provisions; benefit schedules; and financing arrangements. Disability, death, and surviving spouse benefits will not be examined in this study.[1] Despite a marked trend toward liberalization of these benefits, such coverage is generally less expensive than retirement benefits.

The costs of changing the other contractual arrangements depend on actuarial assumptions that differ from firm to firm and are generally unavailable to those outside the firm. No precise statements concern-

---

[1] These issues are summarized in Skolnik, "Private Pension Plans."

ing such costs are possible without evaluating the details of work force mobility and retirement patterns, funding approaches, worker mortality, and so forth for each firm. We can, however, examine the features which seriously alter the costs of private pension plans and reach judgments concerning the direction of change. The key features—the normal pension service requirements, vesting provisions, and benefit structures—will be discussed in this chapter.[2] The other features that are seriously affected by ERISA will be reviewed in Chapter 5.

Pension Service Requirements

Table 3 shows the normal minimum service requirements (the number of years that must be worked by an employee before he can collect a normal pension) for each of the survey years and for both conventional and pattern plans. A conventional plan is a single employer plan, most typically an arrangement between an employer and nonunionized employees; a pattern plan is customarily union-negotiated. The principal difference between them is that pattern plans pay a flat dollar benefit for each year worked (typically up to some maximum) irrespective of salary history; conventional plans use salary history and, typically, all years of service to determine benefit levels. Table 3 shows that the service requirements have been liberalized substantially since 1956. ERISA will make the requirement more liberal still.

Table 4 shows the percentage of plans requiring five years or less of service. For conventional plans, the percentage rose from 50 percent in 1956 to 71 percent in 1975; for pattern plans, the percentage requiring five years or less service more than tripled.

The effect of the trend in these provisions is to raise the costs to firms of maintaining pension plans by making it easier for employees to qualify for pensions.

Vesting

Vesting gives the worker a contractual claim on pension payments. In the early days of pension plans, firms had great discretion in deciding who would get a pension and who would be denied. Typically, pensions vested only at the discretion of the firm or, perhaps implicitly, at the time of the employee's retirement. This type of discretionary arrangement is no longer permitted. Even before the enactment of ERISA, however, the trend toward specified vesting provisions was

---

[2] A less comprehensive analysis of these features and a summary of others may be found in ibid.

TABLE 3
Normal Service Requirements

Minimum Service Requirement (years)	1975 Pattern	1975 Conventional	1970 Pattern	1970 Conventional	1965 Pattern	1965 Conventional	1960 Pattern	1960 Conventional	1956 Pattern	1956 Conventional
None	7	32	7	21	5	18	4	14	6	13
1–3	6	27	4	30	0	0	0	0	0	0
5	10	12	5	10	3[a]	42[a]	6	42[a]	1	37
10	62	21	57	26	55	24	49	22	46	29
15	15	7	26	11	33	10	38	16	43	14
20	0	1	1	2	4[b]	6[b]	3[b]	6[b]	4	7

[a] Several of these plans require five years or less.
[b] Several of these plans require sixteen years or more.
SOURCE: Bankers' Trust Co., *Survey of Industrial Retirement Plans*, various issues.

TABLE 4

Minimum Service for Pension Eligibility: Percentage of Plans
Requiring Five or Less Years of Service

Year	Pattern	Conventional
1956	7	50
1960	10	56
1965	8	60
1970	16	61
1975	23	71

Source: Bankers' Trust Co., *Survey of Industrial Retirement Plans*, various issues.

quite pronounced, and the trend had been away from vesting only at the time of retirement.

Table 5 shows the percentage of firms with specified contractual vesting provisions. All plans, both pattern and conventional, now specify the contractual obligation of the firm, and vesting typically occurs under current contractual arrangements long before retirement.

As Table 6 shows, in the 1956 survey 25 percent of conventional and 59 percent of pattern plans had no vesting provision or vesting only at retirement. Of those that did have vesting provisions, most plans had both an age and service requirement. By 1975 most firms had only service requirements.

In 1956, 21 percent of conventional plans had only service requirements, but no pattern plans did. Vesting occurred upon retirement. By 1975, 68 percent of pattern plans had only service requirements compared with 57 percent of conventional plans. As pattern plans moved to specific vesting provisions, they moved very quickly

TABLE 5

Percentage of Pension Plans with Vesting Provisions

Year	Pattern	Conventional
1956	41	74
1960	82	90
1965	94	97
1970	99	98
1975	100	100

Source: Bankers' Trust Co., *Survey of Industrial Retirement Plans*, various issues.

TABLE 6

Detailed Vesting Provisions

(percentage of plans)

Vesting	1975 Pattern	1975 Conventional	1970 Pattern	1970 Conventional	1965 Pattern	1965 Conventional	1960 Pattern	1960 Conventional	1956 Pattern	1956 Conventional
Service										
10 yrs. or less	56	38	34	21	10	12	4	6	0	8
15 yrs.	6	12	6	11	1	10	0	8	0	5
20 yrs.	6	5	4	8	0	7	0	10	0	8
25 yrs.	0	2	0	2	0	1	0	0	0	0
Subtotal	68	57	44	42	11	30	4	24	0	21
Age										
55	0	2	1	3	0	2	0	2	0	3
60	0	0	0	1	0	1	0	2	0	2
Subtotal	0	2	1	4	0	3	0	4	0	5

5 to 25 years of service and attainment of age										
35	4	3	3	2	0	0	0	0	0	0
40	25	20	34	13	63	12	37	7	17	4
45	3	8	5	11	6	14	9	11	0	6
50	0	3	4	7	4	13	1	11	0	11
55	0	4	3	14	3	14	10	15	3	13
60	0	1	4	3	6	7	10	11	13	8
Subtotal	32	39	53	50	82	60	67	55	33	42
Partial vesting	0	2	1	2	1	4	3	7	4	6
Other	0	0	0	0	0	0	8	0	4	1
No vesting	0	0	1	2	6	3	18	10	59	25
Subtotal	0	2	2	4	7	7	21	17	67	32
Total	100	100	100	100	100	100	100	100	100	100

SOURCE: Bankers' Trust Co., *Survey of Industrial Retirement Plans*, various issues.

through the intermediate category of both age and service requirements. Conventional plans, starting with relatively less stringent vesting provisions, now have relatively more stringent vesting requirements. Thus vesting provisions for union-represented employees are more liberal than for their counterparts (mostly nonunion employees) in conventional plans.

As vesting requirements become less stringent, the firm's pension costs should increase, other things equal,[3] because a higher portion of the work force will reach vested status. Total pension contributions of the firm will be larger than otherwise.

Pension Benefits

One pension benefit issue has to do with who pays for it—the employer or the employee. In large measure, this is a bookkeeping issue for, no matter how financed, the contributions arise from employee productivity and the cost savings achieved by the firm as a result of employee incentive.

Contributions to the pension fund are sometimes made entirely by the employer (noncontributory plans) and sometimes partially by the employee (contributory plans). In some instances employee contributions are mandatory while in others they are voluntary. In typical contributory plans, the employee's portion of the combined contribution, but not the employer's portion, is refunded if employment is terminated prior to vesting.

Table 7 shows that in 1956 most plans required employee contributions, but in 1975, 67 percent were noncontributory and more than half the remaining contributory plans did not require employees to contribute anything directly.

The trend away from employee contributions is consistent with the trend toward less stringent vesting requirements. In 1956 the stringency of vesting requirements was eased by the fact that mandatory contributions could be returned to employees upon their premature departure. Even if employees left before vesting, they could get some funds from the plan and would have enjoyed the benefit of the income tax shield on the pension contributions they made during their employment. Many employers allowed employees to transfer their pension accounts to other firms, thus preserving the tax benefits. For those who were unable to transfer, the immediate tax burden

---

[3] Changes in vesting requirements could induce firms to increase labor turnover to the point that the percentage of employees achieving vested status remains unchanged. Given the increase in labor turnover in recent years, there is at least a possibility that this has occurred.

TABLE 7

CONTRIBUTIONS BY EMPLOYEES TO PENSION FUNDS

(percentage of plans)

| Year | Noncontributory | Contributory | |
		Mandatory	Voluntary
1956	45	54	1
1960	45	54	1
1965	50	39	11
1970	56	28	16
1975	67	14	19

NOTE: Over the years the way plans have been categorized has been somewhat changed. These changes were modest and do not seriously affect the obvious trend.

SOURCE: Bankers' Trust Co., *Survey of Industrial Retirement Plans*, various issues.

could be quite high; whether they enjoyed a net tax advantage would depend on their current and previous tax brackets. Even with the taxes on the lump-sum payment, employees might still have benefited from the arrangement and would definitely have benefited if they were fired with no good prospects for reemployment. As vesting requirements have become less stringent, employers may feel somewhat less pressure to use the mandatory contribution approach: there is a higher probability, other things being equal, that employees will achieve vested status. The percentage of plans with voluntary, as opposed to mandatory, contributions has probably grown as a result of the provision for income tax deferrals on pension fund contributions.

As I shall show later in this chapter this change in pension financing has not seriously altered benefit schedules, reflecting a somewhat arbitrary categorization of plans as noncontributory and mandatory contributory in the absence of vesting considerations.

A second important aspect of the benefit structure is the basis for compensation. Typically, pension benefits are determined by use of a formula that takes account of the number of years of service, the historical compensation or salary of the employee, and some percentage specified in the plan. A simple formulation that takes no account of integration with the social security system might be:

$$\text{Annual pension benefit} =$$
$$\text{Salary basis} \times \text{number of years of service} \times 0.015.$$

The percentage and the salary basis used differ greatly among firms.

TABLE 8

COMPENSATION BASIS OF CONVENTIONAL PLANS

(percentage of plans)

Compensation Basis	1975	1970	1965	1960	1956
All benefits based on career average salary	22	35	45	56	62
All benefits based on final average salary	54	39	31	27	26
Regular benefits based on career average compensation; minimum pension based on final average	16	20	16	12	6
Benefits based partly on career average, partly on final average	8	6	8	5	6

SOURCE: Bankers' Trust Co., *Survey of Industrial Retirement Plans*, various issues.

Some firms examine the entire earnings history of an employee, compute the arithmetic average, and use that as the compensation basis. Others consider only salary from the last several years or choose an amalgam of the two. Table 8 gives a breakdown of these differences and reveals that since 1956 the use of career average salaries has declined markedly in favor of approaches utilizing final averages.

Although career average plans would normally yield benefits identical to those of final average plans, during periods of high unanticipated inflation they lead to lower relative benefits because the nominal wage rises more rapidly than the real wage. In view of the considerable secular inflation in the United States since the Korean War, the shift to plans which give greater weight to final pay is not surprising because it tends to keep the real value of pension benefits relatively stable.

Table 9 shows that final pay was more heavily weighted than career pay in 78 percent of the pension plans surveyed in 1975, compared with 38 percent in 1956; it also shows a strong trend toward shortening the period over which final pay average is computed. In 1956 less than a third of the plans with final pay formulas considered the final five or fewer years; by 1975 this had grown to 95 percent. While this trend may have many causes, inflation has been a principal factor. By focusing on final nominal pay, firms are providing some protection from inflation to employees who are nearing retirement.

If the nominal value of pension fund equity assets as well as the nominal value of contributions rose with inflation, the real costs of the

TABLE 9

Salary Used in Benefit Formulas in Conventional Plans

Year	Percent of Total Using Final Pay Formulas	Percent of Final Pay Formulas Using Average of	
		5 years or less	5 years or more
1956	38	32	68
1960	44	53	47
1965	55	57	43
1970	65	78	22
1975	78	95	5

Source: Bankers' Trust Co., *Survey of Industrial Retirement Plans*, various issues.

pension program would not vary with the salary basis of the pension fund benefit. However, if the nominal value of the pension fund assets does not rise with inflation, the final pay formula could impose an unanticipated burden on the firms offering such arrangements. Unfortunately, in recent years equity values have not kept pace with inflation. Therefore, as firms' pension obligations have grown—in part because of the final pay arrangements—the pension fund asset base has shrunk in real terms.[4] The switch to final pay from career average plans has resulted in real costs to firms that are higher than anticipated, and this situation will persist as long as financial markets are depressed.[5]

Benefit Levels Over Time

Tables 10, 11, 12, and 13 show the changes that have occurred in the benefit structure since 1956.

Table 10 shows median replacement ratios—the amount of pension benefit divided by the final year's salary—from private retirement plans and from social security benefits for the survey years 1956, 1960, 1965, 1970, and 1975. When social security benefits are combined with private pension benefits, higher-paid employees receive a lower

---

[4] See Jeffrey F. Jaffe and Gershon Madelker, "The 'Fisher Effect' for Risky Assets: An Empirical Investigation," *Journal of Finance*, vol. 31 (May 1976), pp. 447–458. Although it is not known how the value of pension fund assets has been affected by inflation, the changes have probably been similar to the changes in the value of financial assets in general.

[5] Further evidence on this appears in Table 11 of this chapter.

TABLE 10

MEDIAN REPLACEMENT RATIOS OF CONVENTIONAL PLANS, WITH AND WITHOUT SOCIAL SECURITY

(percent of final salary)

Year	Salary schedule and Benefit	Final Salary[a] Low	Medium (1)	Medium (2)	High
1975	Salary schedule	$9,000	$15,000	$25,000	$50,000
	Private pension	29.0	32.0	35.0	38.0
	Social security	39.0	25.0	15.0	8.0
	Total	68.0	57.0	50.0	46.0
1970	Salary schedule	$6,000	$12,000	$20,000	$40,000
	Private pension	31.5	41.5	41.5	46.5
	Social security	31.4	16.5	9.9	5.0
	Total	62.9	58.0	51.4	51.5
1965	Salary schedule	$4,500	$8,000	$15,000	$35,000
	Private pension	30.8	38.6	41.4	46.4
	Social security	32.3	19.1	10.2	4.4
	Total	63.1	57.7	51.6	50.8
1960	Salary schedule	$4,000	$7,000	$15,000	$30,000
	Private pension	26.1	34.2	39.2	39.2
	Social security	33.6	21.8	10.2	5.1
	Total	59.7	56.0	49.4	44.3
1956	Salary schedule	$3,000	$4,200	$7,200	$20,000
	Private pension	28.0	28.0	36.6	41.6
	Social security	35.4	31.0	18.1	6.5
	Total	63.4	59.0	54.7	48.1

[a] Final salaries assume 5 percent growth rate and thirty years of service.

SOURCE: Bankers' Trust Co., *Survey of Industrial Retirement Plans*, various issues.

percentage of their final salary in retirement benefits than do lower-paid employees. However, the replacement ratios from private benefits are absolutely and proportionally better for higher-paid employees than for lower-paid employees. Social security payments account for the disparity.

Wage replacement from social security benefits varies inversely with final salary. For low-paid workers ($9,000 in 1975), replacement ratios ranged from a low of 31.4 percent in 1970 to a high of 39.0 percent in 1975. For high-paid workers ($50,000 in 1975), the variation in social security replacement ratios was larger, ranging from 4.4 in 1965 to 8.0 percent in 1975.

Perhaps the most important finding shown in Table 10 is that for conventional plans total pension replacement ratios have not changed much. For low-paid employees, it has ranged from 59.7 to 68.0 percent; for the two mid-ranges in final salary it has ranged from 56.0 to 59.0 percent and from 49.7 to 54.7 percent, respectively; and for high final salary the range has been 44.3 to 51.5 percent. These figures, particularly those for lower-paid employees, compare quite favorably with replacement ratios that various researchers suggest are necessary to maintain the same standard of living in retirement as workers enjoyed before.[6]

The lack of a substantial upward drift in median replacement ratios indicates that the rising pension costs have been the result not of changes in the pension benefit structures of firms, but of the expansion in the number of workers eligible for pension benefits. This would be partly a result of the relaxation of vesting requirements.

Table 11 shows median replacement ratios of private pension plans according to the two compensation bases used in the benefit formulas. From 1956 to 1970 career average plans tended to be a little more generous than final salary plans. In the 1975 survey, however, final pay plans became more generous and, if high inflation persists, will probably continue to be so. If the formulas were indexed, career average plans could be made equivalent to final pay plans because past salaries would rise with inflation. Problems for firms arise when the nominal value of pension fund assets does not keep pace with inflation. Annual contributions then have to be increased to offset the decline in the real value of the assets. Because final salary plans are a type of partial indexing for inflation, using this approach could result in unanticipated burdens on firms.[7]

Table 12 shows the average annual retirement benefits of pattern plans per year of service. Since 1956 both the average annual benefit per year of service and the maximum allowable years of service have

---

[6] James H. Schulz argues that replacement should approximate 60 to 65 percent of final five years' earnings to keep living standards unchanged (*The Economics of Aging*, p. 72). This reduction of income is appropriate because of lower tax burdens, no job-related expenses, and in-kind transfers that are available to the elderly.

[7] From 1970 to 1974, a period during which inflation was unexpectedly high in the United States, 71 percent of conventional plans and 72 percent of pattern plans granted increases in pension benefits to employees who had already retired. These firms apparently perceived themselves as better able to assume the risk of uncertain inflation than their retired employees.

43

TABLE 11

MEDIAN REPLACEMENT RATIOS OF CONVENTIONAL PLANS BY COMPENSATION BASIS

(percent of final salary)

Year	Compensation Basis	Percent of Plans for Each Basis	Final Salary[a]			
			Low	Medium (1)	Medium (2)	High
1975	Career average	22	28	31	35	37
	Final salary	78	30	33	36	38
1970	Career average	35	36–40	46–50	46–50	51–55
	Final salary	65	26–30	36–40	36–40	41–45
1965	Career average	56	31–35	41–45	46–50	51–55
	Final salary	44	26–30	31–35	31–35	36–40
1960	Career average	62	26–30	36–40	41–45	41–45
	Final salary	38	21–25	26–30	31–35	31–35
1956	Career average	72	26–30	26–30	36–40	41–45
	Final salary	28	26–30	26–30	31–35	36–40

[a] Salary schedules are the same as shown in Table 10; a 5 percent growth rate and thirty years of service are assumed.

SOURCE: Bankers' Trust Co., *Survey of Industrial Retirement Plans,* various issues.

risen. This means that a retired employee receives more for each year of service, and more years of service are counted. In 1956 only seventeen of forty-six plans placed no limit on creditable service; in 1975 forty-three of fifty-two placed no such limit. In addition, in the no-limit category, average annual benefits per year of service rose from $24 to $108. This represents a substantial rise, even in real terms, and the same is true across the board. For example, in nominal terms average annual retirement benefits for pattern plans rose from $20 per year of service in 1956 to $106 per year of service in 1975. In real 1970 dollars, average annual benefits rose from approximately $29.50 to roughly $76.20 per year of service.

Table 13 reveals the same phenomenon for replacement ratios of pattern plans. In 1956 most retired employees were receiving at most 14 percent replacement from corporate pensions. By 1975 most employees in pattern plans could achieve replacement as high as 32 percent. This rapid rise in potential replacement plus the liberalization

TABLE 12

AVERAGE ANNUAL RETIREMENT BENEFITS OF PATTERN PLANS

Year	Number of Pattern Plans[a]	Average Annual Benefit per Year of Service (dollars)	Maximum Credited Service[b] (dollars per year of service rounded to nearest dollar)				
			25 years or less	30 years	35 years	40 years	No limit
1956	46	20	20 (5)	19 (19)	14 (5)	0	24 (17)
1960	48	26	0	25 (12)	27 (9)	0	26 (27)
1965	45	35	0	28 (3)	31 (9)	0	37 (33)
1970	43	55	0	35 (5)	55 (1)	60 (2)	58 (35)
1975	52	106	0	103 (3)	90 (5)	110 (1)	108 (43)

[a] Where the source shows benefits as possibly varying from a known amount, those plans are ignored.

[b] Number of plans in each category appears in parentheses.

SOURCE: Bankers' Trust Co., *Survey of Industrial Retirement Plans*, various issues.

of vesting requirements has resulted in much higher costs for pattern plans. Pattern plans appear to have grown relatively more generous than conventional plans.

Pension Plan Cost Trends

Patrick Regan has examined the actual pension cost trends for a small sample of very large firms (see Table 14).[8] Of the forty firms included in his sample, only five are not among the 100 largest U.S. corporations. Thirteen of the forty firms are represented in the thirty Dow Jones Industrial companies. The forty firms employ 5.1 million people

---

[8] Patrick J. Regan, *The 1976 BEA Pension Survey* (New York: BEA Associates, 1976).

TABLE 13

Median Replacement Ratios of Pattern Plans

(percent of final salary)

	Service				
Year	25 years and less	30 years[a]	35 years	40 years	No limit[b]
1956	12	14	12	0	26
1960	0	11	14	0	17
1965	0	11	14	0	21
1970	0	9	16	20	22
1975	0	21	21	29	32

[a] For comparison with Table 10, the relevant column is 30 years of service.

[b] When there was no limit to service, it was arbitrarily set at 45 years. It was felt that this represented, on average, the maximum number of years that could be expected from a worker.

NOTE: Final salary levels for each year are medium (1) levels taken from the salary schedule of Table 10. Replacement ratios were obtained by multiplying the dollar amount found in Table 12 times the years of service and then dividing by the final salary level.

SOURCE: Tables 10 and 12.

—approximately 15 percent of the employees covered by industrial pension plans in the United States. These firms' pension fund assets account for slightly more than 20 percent of total private uninsured pension fund assets.

Table 14 shows that total pension fund costs have risen from 1969 to 1975 at rather substantial rates; between 1971 and 1975 they rose by 12.0 to 19.5 percent per year. One possible reason for this might be that these firms were growing over the period and adding new employees at a rapid rate, but per employee costs were also rising. Of course it was a period of relatively severe inflation, but annual pension fund contributions are determined by long-run actuarial estimates and should be relatively unaffected by a short period of extremely rapid unanticipated change in the aggregate price level. Another possible explanation is that the firms in the sample may have chosen to pay down their unfunded past service costs and unfunded vested benefits. However, there is no evidence that this was done to any appreciable extent, even though under the new requirements of ERISA those firms with large unfunded liabilities must eliminate them over the next forty years. It thus appears that the increase in costs was

TABLE 14

GROWTH IN PENSION COSTS OF FORTY COMPANIES

(percent of companies in each range)

Growth Range	1975	1974	1973	1972	1971	1970	1969
Negative	12.5	7.5	7.5	12.5	7.5	22.5	17.5
0 to 5 percent	10.0	0.0	10.0	12.5	12.5	10.0	20.0
5 to 10 percent	5.0	10.0	10.0	17.5	10.0	17.5	27.5
10 to 15 percent	22.5	10.0	22.5	12.5	22.5	5.0	10.0
15 to 20 percent	7.5	22.5	10.0	10.0	2.5	12.5	5.0
20 to 25 percent	20.0	7.5	12.5	7.5	15.0	10.0	7.5
25 to 40 percent	17.5	30.0	17.5	22.5	20.0	10.0	10.0
40 percent and over	5.0	12.5	10.0	5.0	10.0	12.5	2.5
Total	100.0	100.0	100.0	100.0	100.0	100.0	100.0
Median annual growth rate of pension costs	14.7	19.5	14.5	12.0	14.0	10.5	7.0

NOTE: See Table 17 for the names of the companies considered.

SOURCE: Patrick J. Regan, *The 1976 BEA Pension Survey* (New York: BEA Associates, 1976), table 2, p. 6.

TABLE 15

PENSION COSTS OF FORTY COMPANIES AS A PERCENTAGE OF FUNDS
AVAILABLE AND OF PRETAX PROFITS, 1975

Range of Costs	Pension Costs as Percentage of Funds Available[a]		Pension Costs as Percentage of Pretax Profits	
	Number of firms	Percentage of firms	Number of firms	Percentage of firms
0 to 5 percent	2	5.0	2	5.0
5 to 10 percent	8	20.0	7	17.5
10 to 15 percent	8	20.0	8	20.5
15 to 20 percent	2	5.0	2	5.0
20 to 25 percent	6	15.0	3	7.5
25 to 40 percent	7	17.5	7	17.5
40 percent and over	7	17.5	11	27.5
Total	40	100.0	40	100.0
Median (percent)	18.5		22	

[a] "Funds available" are pretax profits plus pension costs.
NOTE: See Table 17 for the names of the companies considered.
SOURCE: Patrick J. Regan, *The 1976 BEA Pension Survey* (New York: BEA Associates, 1976), table 4, p. 10.

caused mainly by changes in pension contracts—liberalization of service and vesting requirements and benefits.

Table 15 shows pension costs as a percentage of pretax profits and as a percentage of funds available (pretax profits plus pension costs) in 1975. For the group of forty firms, the median pension cost was 22 percent of pretax profits and 18.5 percent of pretax profits plus pension costs. According to Regan, in 1975 the growth rate in pension costs remained within its normal historical range. Given the firms' own contractual arrangements and the cost of meeting the new rules of ERISA, however, these costs may rise further still and become burdensome.

Another factor affecting pension costs is the financial performance of pension fund assets. If the value of pension fund assets, predominantly common stocks, rises by more than anticipated in the actuarial estimates which form the basis of pension funding policy, then the real transfers from the firms to their pension funds may be cut. Regan estimates that if pension fund performance consistently exceeded the assumed return by 1 percent, pretax profits would rise on average by 4 to 5 percent for the pension-sponsoring firms.[9] Unfortunately, the performance of pension fund assets depends largely on the performance of U.S. equity markets, and these markets have performed dismally in recent years.

Table 16 is based on the annual reports of the sample firms and the Form 10-K that each is required to file with the U.S. Securities and Exchange Commission. It shows the average total cost of the pension plan per employee for the forty firms for 1965 and 1970 through 1976. Total cost includes not only the firm's actual per employee contribution to the pension plan, but also the per employee increase in unfunded past service obligations and unfunded vested benefits.[10] For comparative purposes, actual average employer contributions to the social security program are also shown. Both have climbed substantially, and this would be true even if inflation were taken into account. (Tables 17–21 at the end of this chapter give the raw data upon which this table is based.)

The Burden of Social Security

The intent of levying half the social security tax on the employer and half on the employee was to divide the tax burden equally, but in effect the burden of the firm's social security tax payment is probably borne by the employee eventually.[11] If there were no social security tax, employees' salaries would be higher by the amount paid by the employer or, alternatively, the prices of the goods purchased by the employee as consumer would be less by that amount. Whether the tax is fully shifted to the employee or shifted forward to the consumer, the net effect is that it is not borne wholly by the owners of the firm—the tax does not affect profits. While this may hold over the long run, it may not hold over the short run when increases in social security payments are unanticipated.

---

[9] Ibid., p. 2.

[10] These data are a little crude. Some firms give the average number of employees during the year, others give year-end figures. In addition, some firms report both unfunded past service obligations and unfunded vested benefits, whereas others report one or the other. In compiling the data, however, I have been consistent across time. That is, if a firm began the period by reporting only one of these figures and concluded by reporting both, the data which had no earlier counterpart were excluded. This makes the data comparable across years, even though slightly biased. In any event, since we are interested in identifying broad trends, precision is principally important with respect to comparability over time.

[11] See Alicia H. Munnell, *The Future of Social Security* (Washington, D.C.: Brookings Institution, 1977), pp. 85–88 and references cited there.

TABLE 16

AVERAGE PENSION AND SOCIAL SECURITY PAYMENTS PER YEAR AND PER EMPLOYEE FOR FORTY COMPANIES

Payment and Percent Change	1965	1970	1971	1972	1973	1974	1975	1976
Average pension payments (dollars)	287.52	395.67	455.51	516.56	588.53	718.72	841.03	1,146.84
Percent change	N.A.	6.5[a]	15.12	13.4	13.93	22.12	17.02	36.36
Average social security payment (dollars)	136.27	259.61	286.81	331.34	415.89	488.23	545.25	600.10
Percent change	N.A.	14.0[a]	9.48	15.53	26.13	17.39	11.68	10.06
Total payments (dollars)	423.79	655.28	742.32	846.29	1,004.42	1,206.95	1,386.28	1,746.94
Percent change	N.A.	9.0[a]	13.28	14.01	18.69	20.16	14.86	26.02

N.A.: Not available.
[a] These figures will produce the five-year geometric average for 1965–1970.
SOURCE: Tables 17–21.

Table 16 shows that over the past several years the average employer contribution to social security per employee for the forty-firm sample has risen dramatically. If these increases were not fully anticipated, firms would probably not have been able to shift fully and immediately these tax increases to either employees or customers. As a result, profits would be reduced by the growth in social security taxes.

TABLE 17

TOTAL NUMBER OF EMPLOYEES OF FORTY U.S. COMPANIES

Company	1965	1970	1971	1972	1973	1974	1975	1976
American Home Products	30,567	42,000	42,000	44,000	45,000	45,700	46,400	47,600
American Motors	32,000	22,769	23,991	25,469	32,700	34,700	33,200	29,500
Armco Steel	38,006	51,236	50,000	50,000	52,000	52,000	49,000	49,000
Babcock & Wilcox	37,000	36,528	36,526	34,473	37,748	40,075	40,975	39,454
Beatrice Foods	19,672	N.A.	58,000	62,000	65,000	64,000	67,000	N.A.
Bethlehem Steel	130,000	130,000	115,000	109,000	118,000	122,000	113,000	105,000
Borden	N.A.	46,000	48,000	46,700	46,500	46,700	42,100	40,400
Caterpillar Tractor	50,800	64,000	60,500	66,576	74,431	80,144	78,286	77,793
Chrysler	166,773	228,000	228,000	245,000	274,000	256,000	217,000	245,000
Combustion Engineering	22,800	31,604	33,000	34,734	35,316	40,765	45,938	42,843
Dow Chemical	33,800	47,400	47,800	48,800	49,800	52,300	53,100	53,000
DuPont	106,013	110,685	106,593	111,052	118,423	136,866	132,235	132,737
Eastman Kodak	88,400	110,700	109,700	114,800	120,700	124,100	124,000	127,000
Firestone	88,000	90,000	106,000	109,000	117,000	120,000	111,000	113,000
Ford	364,487	431,727	433,074	442,607	474,318	464,731	416,120	443,917
General Electric	257,903	397,000	363,000	369,000	388,000	404,000	375,000	380,000
General Foods	30,000	46,700	48,500	48,000	47,000	48,000	47,000	N.A.
General Motors	735,000	696,000	773,000	760,000	811,000	734,000	681,000	748,000
B. F. Goodrich	43,884	48,000	55,800	50,600	51,900	48,900	45,000	39,200
Goodyear	103,644	136,000	140,300	149,700	155,400	151,975	149,150	152,600
Honeywell	54,634	100,230	94,420	96,650	98,122	92,173	83,053	70,775
IBM	172,445	269,291	265,493	262,152	274,108	292,350	288,647	291,977

Johnson & Johnson	19,600	38,200	40,000	43,300	49,100	54,300	53,800	57,900
Kraftco	45,157	48,000	48,000	48,900	48,900	50,400	48,400	N.A.
Kresge	45,000	81,000	93,000	112,000	125,000	134,000	155,000	N.A.
Lockheed	81,302	84,600	74,700	69,600	66,900	62,100	57,600	55,100
Monsanto	56,227	63,000	59,000	58,000	58,000	61,000	59,250	61,900
J. C. Penney	63,000	145,000	162,000	175,000	200,000	193,000	186,000	N.A.
Pfizer	30,000	33,000	33,800	36,500	37,400	39,500	39,200	40,081
Republic Steel	55,888	47,726	42,951	40,939	43,803	44,230	39,430	39,593
Sears	290,000	395,806	401,883	417,895	439,493	425,000	417,000	N.A.
Sperry Rand	93,596	87,401	85,574	91,345	98,777	92,963	87,090	N.A.
Union Carbide	73,900	102,144	99,181	98,114	109,417	109,566	106,475	113,000
Uniroyal	64,958	64,168	63,736	64,466	64,402	63,845	55,542	N.A.
United States Steel	209,000	200,734	182,940	176,486	184,794	187,503	172,796	166,645
Warner-Lambert	16,900	55,000	56,000	56,000	59,000	58,500	57,500	58,000
Western Union	26,485	23,735	19,550	17,329	15,200	15,000	13,982	13,492
Westinghouse	128,131	186,313	180,299	183,768	194,100	199,248	166,000	160,945
F. W. Woolworth	86,000	100,000	110,000	115,000	100,000	100,000	90,000	N.A.
Xerox	15,758	59,862	66,728	75,923	94,036	101,380	93,530	97,336

N.A.: Not available.

NOTES: In Tables 17–21, restated figures were used for the following companies: Western Union, Chrysler, Westinghouse, Honeywell, Borden, General Electric, Combustion Engineering, Beatrice Foods, and J. C. Penney.

The following companies had year ends other than December 31: American Motors, September 30; Firestone, October 31; Beatrice Foods, February 28; General Foods and Sperry Rand, March 31; J.C. Penney and Kresge, January 30; Johnson & Johnson, January 31, 1971, but December 31 for all other years.

The pension data for Sears and J. C. Penney includes both pension and profit-sharing contributions. The data for American Home Products includes retirement, group life, sickness and accident, and medical expense insurance plans.

Because of their unreliability, the following data were excluded from the computation of average per year, per employee social security contributions: Western Union, 1965; Uniroyal, 1965, 1970, 1971, 1972, 1973, 1974, 1975; Monsanto, 1972; General Electric, 1965; Combustion Engineering, 1970, 1971, 1972, 1973; Beatrice Foods, 1972; American Home Products, 1965.

SOURCES: Corporate Annual Reports; U.S. Securities and Exchange Commission Forms 10-K; and Compustat tapes of Standard and Poor's Corporation.

TABLE 18

Total Corporate Pension Contributions of Forty U.S. Companies

(thousands of dollars)

Company	1965	1970	1971	1972	1973	1974	1975	1976
American Home Products	8,056	6,758	7,344	6,683	8,673	7,068	8,042	5,079
American Motors	9,200	15,386	16,521	17,654	20,927	24,762	28,666	37,036
Armco Steel	16,317	25,101	25,275	33,664	46,381	54,824	63,054	82,889
Babcock & Wilcox	6,700	11,307	13,872	20,054	22,761	26,257	32,236	33,400
Beatrice Foods	1,859	4,400	4,500	7,700	17,990	20,490	14,790	N.A.
Bethlehem Steel	28,260	46,686	56,603	80,919	115,533	153,842	198,400	261,200
Borden	4,729	4,644	4,819	4,644	6,830	8,300	10,400	14,500
Caterpillar Tractor	20,300	33,000	46,100	56,400	61,700	88,600	106,900	100,300
Chrysler	85,300	121,406	148,900	147,300	161,700	212,800	233,100	277,100
Combustion Engineering	3,632	8,548	10,494	11,608	14,001	16,688	21,381	26,063
Dow Chemical	12,873	17,177	20,580	24,966	29,684	65,406	65,708	82,708
DuPont	70,000	94,531	96,100	107,300	101,300	150,100	185,100	212,800
Eastman Kodak	41,800	57,700	56,500	74,500	112,400	118,800	146,700	164,300
Firestone	15,730	33,307	37,077	36,425	39,976	51,030	56,373	60,056
Ford	157,498	160,500	239,200	312,100	335,900	385,300	426,700	505,500
General Electric	43,200	66,600	91,000	107,600	135,500	167,800	193,100	240,100
General Foods	7,925	8,532	15,943	20,711	20,423	18,865	26,166	34,340
General Motors	225,000	329,000	584,000	639,700	718,700	818,600	969,100	1,071,200
B. F. Goodrich	10,250	16,700	22,800	24,620	36,000	39,650	40,475	40,650
Goodyear	23,890	48,565	55,528	57,404	59,371	79,295	96,764	87,692

Honeywell	7,450	27,506	26,256	28,303	29,280	41,522	37,600	50,200
IBM	50,590	133,000	170,000	221,000	258,000	334,000	419,000	590,000
Johnson & Johnson	3,840	8,816	9,712	11,590	13,310	15,683	21,298	28,888
Kraftco	7,905	16,450	18,000	19,525	19,650	22,875	28,550	N.A.
Kresge	2,170	4,721	5,363	6,814	8,696	11,547	18,253	N.A.
Lockheed	41,398	65,000	76,000	80,000	79,000	100,000	77,000	96,000
Monsanto	25,500	31,845	36,300	35,900	35,900	47,200	57,300	70,700
J. C. Penney	12,658	19,509	23,491	31,242	33,049	30,079	40,200	N.A.
Pfizer	1,330	6,200	9,200	10,900	11,700	15,700	19,800	20,800
Republic Steel	10,931	32,445	33,305	42,002	50,884	55,015	66,562	83,784
Sears	63,128	96,957	95,044	114,449	126,413	138,917	110,994	112,783
Sperry Rand	N.A.	25,000	34,000	34,000	46,600	54,800	52,000	N.A.
Union Carbide	27,418	39,825	44,500	46,000	64,100	87,200	96,800	130,300
Uniroyal	22,607	41,091	45,256	47,837	53,415	64,225	69,409	N.A.
United States Steel	34,600	104,804	62,118	73,530	89,994	169,900	215,800	221,000
Warner-Lambert	2,690	11,500	15,366	16,542	20,537	24,069	25,355	29,318
Western Union	12,768	20,831	21,631	18,742	29,988	32,403	31,844	33,442
Westinghouse	13,300	31,600	43,100	48,700	60,376	75,200	66,200	108,500
F. W. Woolworth	6,020	10,333	10,762	10,842	12,151	13,712	16,533	18,900
Xerox	13,954	53,237	60,904	81,059	92,163	97,416	66,681	105,823

N.A.: Not available.
NOTES AND SOURCES: Same as Table 17.

TABLE 19

Total Corporate Social Security Contributions of Forty U.S. Companies

(thousands of dollars)

Company	1965	1970	1971	1972	1973	1974	1975	1976
American Home Products	6,305	12,996	14,835	17,636	22,672	27,256	29,760	34,305
American Motors	N.A.	11,816	13,231	16,200	23,487	29,163	27,975	30,017
Armco Steel	6,714	20,560	22,532	26,236	36,359	42,526	44,526	49,622
Babcock & Wilcox	N.A.	N.A.	16,750	18,553	24,587	30,816	33,433	35,500
Beatrice Foods	N.A.	15,271	23,076	29,158	37,700	43,003	50,671	N.A.
Bethlehem Steel	N.A.	N.A.	N.A.	N.A.	92,178	106,470	106,900	108,600
Borden	N.A.	14,164	15,989	17,430	N.A.	N.A.	N.A.	N.A.
Caterpillar Tractor	N.A.	29,070	30,616	36,668	56,400	72,100	84,700	89,100
Chrysler	N.A.	N.A.	N.A.	N.A.	N.A.	N.A.	N.A.	N.A.
Combustion Engineering	N.A.	12,052	13,386	17,238	23,212	29,552	31,722	36,391
Dow Chemical	N.A.	24,897	32,980	39,973	51,638	61,635	75,957	83,304
DuPont	N.A.	37,045	37,100	42,000	57,200	N.A.	N.A.	N.A.
Eastman Kodak	N.A.	50,230	56,774	71,987	96,264	111,835	120,063	134,858
Firestone	14,970	30,895	36,087	41,991	53,995	63,935	68,570	72,265
Ford	N.A.	183,000	208,000	277,900	358,000	402,400	443,200	557,800
General Electric	45,000	141,300	140,500	167,500	225,800	254,600	264,800	302,200
General Foods	N.A.	15,212	16,276	19,383	N.A.	N.A.	N.A.	N.A.
General Motors	N.A.	N.A.	377,178	466,382	609,927	648,406	669,562	814,400
B. F. Goodrich	N.A.	17,009	18,264	27,381	35,879	40,625	39,014	39,165
Goodyear	N.A.	31,566	35,749	44,077	58,462	61,311	59,886	68,225

Honeywell	N.A.	44,735	49,337	61,526	79,754	80,179	54,167	59,991
IBM	N.A.	141,451	139,883	166,489	220,191	272,631	330,564	370,515
Johnson & Johnson	N.A.	13,474	16,583	21,814	32,408	42,516	52,379	56,912
Kraftco	N.A.	N.A.	13,893	16,761	20,333	22,136	22,789	N.A.
Kresge	N.A.	18,105	24,085	N.A.	N.A.	N.A.	N.A.	N.A.
Lockheed	N.A.	40,563	37,131	43,779	51,970	54,200	54,700	59,500
Monsanto	N.A.	22,390	22,221	27,659	31,900	40,400	42,500	52,000
J. C. Penney	N.A.	39,742	46,142	57,233	69,278	80,595	96,600	N.A.
Pfizer	N.A.	12,803	14,056	18,705	24,062	30,200	36,600	N.A.
Republic Steel	N.A.	21,414	21,317	25,328	36,936	40,734	35,533	42,407
Sears	N.A.	97,286	103,171	116,166	135,703	176,438	N.A.	N.A.
Sperry Rand	N.A.	32,085	34,433	41,762	56,672	67,194	68,555	N.A.
Union Carbide	N.A.	N.A.	35,700	40,500	54,600	68,300	76,000	88,100
Uniroyal	14,606	22,470	26,545	31,992	36,526	41,520	47,594	N.A.
United States Steel	N.A.	88,347	88,233	100,311	145,329	168,900	161,900	180,900
Warner-Lambert	N.A.	16,817	21,141	24,360	31,484	35,586	41,532	43,461
Western Union	5,056	7,466	6,652	7,278	N.A.	N.A.	N.A.	N.A.
Westinghouse	N.A.	84,524	96,466	102,374	122,770	136,440	144,025	146,611
F. W. Woolworth	12,931	20,914	23,422	26,151	37,436	41,144	45,216	N.A.
Xerox	N.A.	25,190	31,602	41,684	63,076	94,995	105,972	119,596

N.A.: Not available.

NOTES AND SOURCES: Same as Table 17.

TABLE 20

AVERAGE CORPORATE PENSION CONTRIBUTION PER EMPLOYEE OF FORTY U.S. COMPANIES

(rounded dollars)

Company	1965	1970	1971	1972	1973	1974	1975	1976
American Home Products	264	161	175	152	193	155	173	107
American Motors	287	676	689	693	640	714	863	1,255
Armco Steel	429	490	505	673	892	1,054	1,287	1,692
Babcock & Wilcox	181	310	380	582	603	655	787	847
Beatrice Foods	94	N.A.	78	124	277	320	221	N.A.
Bethlehem Steel	217	359	492	742	979	1,261	1,756	2,488
Borden	N.A.	101	100	99	147	178	247	359
Caterpillar Tractor	400	516	762	847	829	1,105	1,366	1,289
Chrysler	511	532	653	601	590	831	1,074	1,131
Combustion Engineering	159	270	318	334	396	409	465	608
Dow Chemical	381	362	431	512	596	1,227	1,237	1,561
DuPont	660	854	902	966	855	1,097	1,400	1,603
Eastman Kodak	473	521	515	649	931	957	1,183	1,294
Firestone	179	370	350	334	342	425	508	531
Ford	432	372	552	705	208	829	1,025	1,139
General Electric	167	168	251	292	349	415	515	632
General Foods	264	183	329	431	435	393	557	N.A.
General Motors	306	473	755	842	886	1,115	1,423	1,432
B. F. Goodrich	234	348	409	487	694	811	899	1,037
Goodyear	230	357	396	383	382	522	649	575

Honeywell	136	274	278	293	298	450	453	709
IBM	293	494	640	843	941	1,142	1,452	2,021
Johnson & Johnson	196	231	243	268	271	289	396	499
Kraftco	175	343	375	399	402	454	590	N.A.
Kresge	48	58	58	61	70	86	118	N.A.
Lockheed	509	768	1,017	1,149	1,181	1,610	1,337	1,742
Monsanto	454	506	615	619	619	774	967	1,142
J. C. Penney	201	135	145	179	165	156	216	N.A.
Pfizer	44	188	272	299	313	397	505	519
Republic Steel	196	680	775	1,026	1,162	1,244	1,688	2,116
Sears	218	245	236	274	288	327	266	N.A.
Sperry Rand	N.A.	286	397	372	472	589	597	N.A.
Union Carbide	371	390	449	469	586	796	909	1,153
Uniroyal	348	640	710	742	829	1,006	1,250	N.A.
United States Steel	166	522	338	417	487	906	1,249	1,326
Warner-Lambert	159	209	274	295	348	411	441	505
Western Union	482	878	1,106	1,087	1,973	2,160	2,277	2,479
Westinghouse	104	170	239	265	311	377	399	674
F. W. Woolworth	70	103	98	94	122	137	184	N.A.
Xerox	886	889	913	1,068	980	961	713	1,087
Average per year	288	396	456	517	589	719	841	1,147
Percentage change[a]	N.A.	6.5	15.12	13.4	13.93	22.12	17.02	36.36

[a] This figure will produce the five-year geometric average for 1965–1970.

NOTES AND SOURCES: Same as Table 17.

TABLE 21

AVERAGE CORPORATE SOCIAL SECURITY CONTRIBUTION PER EMPLOYEE OF FORTY U.S. COMPANIES

(rounded dollars)

Company	1965	1970	1971	1972	1973	1974	1975	1976
American Home Products	206	309	353	401	504	596	641	721
American Motors	N.A.	259	276	318	359	420	421	509
Armco Steel	88	201	225	262	350	409	454	N.A.
Babcock & Wilcox	N.A.	N.A.	229	269	326	384	408	450
Beatrice Foods	N.A.	N.A.	398	470	580	672	756	N.A.
Bethlehem Steel	N.A.	N.A.	N.A.	N.A.	391	436	473	517
Borden	N.A.	308	333	373	N.A.	N.A.	N.A.	N.A.
Caterpillar Tractor	N.A.	227	253	275	379	450	541	573
Chrysler	N.A.	N.A.	N.A.	N.A.	N.A.	N.A.	N.A.	N.A.
Combustion Engineering	N.A.	381	406	496	657	725	691	849
Dow Chemical	N.A.	263	345	410	518	578	715	786
DuPont	N.A.	335	348	378	483	N.A.	N.A.	N.A.
Eastman Kodak	N.A.	227	259	314	399	451	484	531
Firestone	170	343	340	385	461	533	618	640
Ford	N.A.	212	240	314	377	433	533	628
General Electric	174	356	387	454	582	630	706	795
General Foods	N.A.	326	336	404	N.A.	N.A.	N.A.	N.A.
General Motors	N.A.	N.A.	244	307	376	442	492	544
B. F. Goodrich	N.A.	177	164	271	346	415	433	500
Goodyear	N.A.	232	255	294	376	403	402	447

Honeywell	N.A.	223	261	318	406	435	326	424
IBM	N.A.	263	263	318	402	466	573	634
Johnson & Johnson	N.A.	176	207	252	330	391	487	491
Kraftco	N.A.	N.A.	289	343	416	439	471	N.A.
Kresge	N.A.	224	259	N.A.	N.A.	N.A.	N.A.	N.A.
Lockheed	N.A.	240	249	315	388	436	475	539
Monsanto	N.A.	355	377	477	550	662	717	840
J. C. Penney	N.A.	274	285	327	346	418	519	N.A.
Pfizer	N.A.	194	208	256	322	382	467	N.A.
Republic Steel	N.A.	224	248	309	422	460	451	536
Sears	N.A.	246	257	278	309	415	N.A.	N.A.
Sperry Rand	N.A.	367	402	457	574	723	787	N.A.
Union Carbide	N.A.	N.A.	360	413	499	623	714	780
Uniroyal	112	175	208	248	284	325	428	N.A.
United States Steel	N.A.	220	240	284	395	450	468	543
Warner-Lambert	N.A.	306	378	435	534	608	722	749
Western Union	191	315	340	420	N.A.	N.A.	N.A.	N.A.
Westinghouse	N.A.	227	268	279	316	342	434	455
F. W. Woolworth	150	209	213	227	374	411	502	506
Xerox	N.A.	210	237	225	335	469	567	614
Average per year	136	260	287	331	416	488	545	600
Percent change[a]	N.A.	14.0	9.48	15.53	26.13	17.39	11.68	10.06

[a] This figure will produce the five-year geometric average for 1965–1970.

NOTES AND SOURCES: Same as Table 17.

5

The Employee Retirement
Income Security Act of 1974
and Corporate Pension Plans

Corporate pension plans were subject to few regulations prior to the enactment of ERISA. The Internal Revenue Service had established guidelines to keep pension plans nondiscriminatory—for instance, it set the magnitude of contributions exempt from income taxation—but there was no comprehensive set of rules governing specific features of private pension plans as there is under ERISA. The act stipulates minimum eligibility standards and vesting requirements; it mandates funding policies; it attempts to tighten the guidelines on fiduciary responsibility and establishes a quasi-governmental agency, the Pension Benefit Guaranty Corporation (PBGC), to guide pension funds and provide pension insurance for firms. In addition, ERISA declares that pension funds have contingent claims against parent firms in the event of pension fund insolvency and that these claims have the same legal status and priority as federal tax liens, senior to all other private corporate debt.

ERISA, in short, changes the nature of pensions in fundamental ways. It implicitly regards the pure deferred wage theory of pensions as correct, even though the pension arrangements which many firms and employees have agreed upon cannot be categorized this way. The act requires many firms to modify their pension plans, but it seems likely that modifications will not always be in the direction apparently desired by ERISA's drafters. Instead, many firms will terminate or reduce the benefits under existing plans, and other firms which had contemplated initiating pension plans may ultimately decide against such action. In addition, some firms may very well switch from defined benefit to defined contribution plans or adopt profit-sharing plans in lieu of regular pension plans. Ironically, ERISA itself makes the termination or non-starting options relatively more attractive. Under Title II employees not covered by private pension plans may establish individual retirement accounts (IRAs), which take advantage of the same type of tax deferrals as those offered by industrial pension plans. IRAs are, therefore, reasonably attractive alternatives to private pensions. Although workers' annual contributions to IRAs are limited to an amount less than would accrue under many corporate plans, the limits on tax deductible contributions to IRAs can be expected to move upward.

Before ERISA became law, pension arrangements differed to an extraordinary degree among firms. ERISA will narrow these differences. It tends to standardize complex financial contracts as well as to reduce employee uncertainty about the value of these contracts. The wide variety of pension arrangements presumably reflected differences among firms and employees in the goals and preferences of pension plans. The particular set of pension arrangements that prevailed between a firm and its employees was probably the "best" set of features that could be agreed upon after explicit or implicit bargaining. The package of features, such as vesting requirements and funding policies, reflected a bargained solution. To the extent that ERISA alters the package of features, it disturbs a noncoercively determined pension arrangement. ERISA forces recontracting, and since the thrust of the legislation seems to favor the employee over the firm's equity holders, firms will probably attempt to recontract in ways outside the scope of ERISA to shift terms in their own favor. This can be done by terminating the plan, by reducing benefits, or, less drastically and perhaps more palatably, by increasing the degree of integration of the plan with the social security system (see Chapter 6). Firms have not yet taken full advantage of the integration privilege. By the time all the adjustments are made, the net effects of ERISA on firms and employees may be very small.

Following a review of the major provisions of ERISA, I shall consider the effect of several of these provisions on specific pension fund contracts with employees and on the financial management of pension plans.

Major Provisions

The primary aims of ERISA are the reduction of employee uncertainty about pension claims and the standardization of pension contracts. It seeks to accomplish this in two ways: (1) by making it easier for employees to qualify and acquire rights to pension benefits, thus tending to reduce or eliminate the recurrence of the hard-luck cases of the 1950s and 1960s in which employees who had worked for firms for, say, forty years were fired just before retirement age and thus received no pension benefits; and (2) by ensuring that the pension plan has sufficient assets to pay pension claims or recourse to sufficient assets through explicit claims on the firm's assets and insurance provided by the PBGC. The burden of compliance with ERISA falls most heavily on defined benefit plans, though defined contribution or money purchase plans will also be affected, particularly by the fiduciary responsibility standards.

Two important provisions of ERISA deal with eligibility for participation in the pension plan and vesting. All employees over twenty-five years of age and with more than one year of service or hired more than five years before the normal retirement age must be included in the plan. A year of service is 1,000 hours. Moreover, if there is a break in service, the employee receives credit for past service after completing a year of service following the break.

Vesting. ERISA prescribed that firms follow one of three vesting rules: (1) full vesting at the end of ten years of employment; (2) graduated vesting, wherein an employee gains a nonforfeitable right to 25 percent of the pension after five years, 5 percent more in each of the following five years, and 10 percent more in each of the eleventh through fifteenth years (in which case, an employee would be 35 percent vested at the end of the seventh year of employment, 50 percent vested at the end of the tenth, and 100 percent vested at the end of fifteen years of employment); and (3) the rule of forty-five. If the employee has completed five years of service and the sum of his or her age and years of service equals forty-five, the employee becomes 50 percent vested. Since 100 percent vesting must be reached within five additional years, each additional year of service merits a 10 percent increase in the nonforfeitable pension rights.

An additional feature of the nonforfeitable right under ERISA is that firms must offer vested employees the option of reduced future retirement benefits in return for which the employee's spouse will receive a retirement benefit in the event that the employee dies before retirement.

Funding. ERISA also affects pension funding policy. For existing plans, past service obligations and unfunded vested liabilities must be reduced within forty years. For new plans or for old plans which increase their liabilities as a result of liberalization of benefits, the amortization must occur within thirty years. In addition, pension fund assets and liabilities must be actuarially determined every three years, and these calculations and the assumptions underlying the calculations must be periodically certified by an actuary acceptable to the Labor and

Treasury Departments. Failure to meet minimum funding standards could result in financial penalties against the sponsor which would not be deductible for income tax purposes.

Insurance. Prior to ERISA, employee's pension claims were against the pension fund, not the firm. The firm is now liable for pension fund deficiencies. If the firm does not have satisfactory private insurance, up to 30 percent of the firm's net worth can be taken by the pension fund or its agent to satisfy pension claims and terminate the plan. The claim against the firm has the same status as a tax lien, hence in the event of bankruptcy (which can be forced by the pension fund's agent, the Pension Benefit Guaranty Corporation), the pension fund's claim against the firm is senior to the claims of secured and unsecured debt holders. Satisfactory private insurance for the pension fund could prevent this. Under ERISA firms are obliged to insure their pension funds either through private insurance or through the Pension Benefit Guaranty Corporation.

A pension plan may be terminated by the PBGC by court order if the plan is deemed unsoundly managed or if it appears that pension benefits cannot be paid when due. If a plan is terminated, the PBGC would then assume responsibility for meeting benefit payments of up to $750 per month per retired employee. It would meet these responsibilities out of the insurance premiums it collects from all participating pension plans. If this source of funds proves inadequate, the firm is wholly liable for the pension fund's deficit, and the PBGC can place a lien against 30 percent of the firm's net worth.[1] As a practical matter, the PBGC may insist upon a declining balance note, rather than forcing the firm into bankruptcy.

Fiduciary Responsibility. ERISA requires new standards of fiduciary responsibility for pension fund managers and requires more extensive reporting and disclosure on the status of pension fund assets, liabilities, and activities. The legislation does not specify what "fiduciary responsibility" means, however, and no one knows what the judicial interpretation of it may be. There has been an extensive debate on standards for such things as satisfactory investment performance and suitable

---

[1] The law leaves the computation of this figure unspecified. It is not clear whether it means book net worth, the market value of the equity, or something like "appraisal value" or intrinsic value, which could differ from an accountant's or economist's view. The market value is the most sensible measurement of corporate value, but it is not directly available for privately owned firms. Although it may be inferred, the courts may discard this type of estimate and insist on book net worth. Nondiscrimination would dictate that the same principle be applied to publicly held firms.

portfolio guidelines.[2] This issue is likely to lead to a great deal of litigation and may ultimately prove the most costly of all ERISA provisions because of the excessive caution it may foster on the part of fund administration.

ERISA's reporting and disclosure requirements are complex and comprehensive. The reports to the Labor and the Treasury Departments and to employees may simply prove too costly for many small firms to justify. Economies of scale may be created where they would otherwise not exist. With these new burdens, these firms may very well decide that the cost of administering the programs plus the cost of the pension plans themselves exceed the benefits to the firms.

A detailed quantitative analysis of all the provisions of ERISA is well beyond the scope of this study. However, the more critical provisions for eligibility and vesting standards, funding, and the pension fund's contingent claim against the net worth of the firm deserve treatment. These features are most likely to cause firms to behave substantially differently in the future than in the past. Other provisions, such as those for diversification of mortality and investment risks through PBGC insurance and for IRA tax benefits, will not be treated in any detail.

Eligibility and Vesting

If pensions in all firms were nothing more than deferred wages, then ERISA would be unnecessary. Private employment contracts would have recognized the employee's immediate claim. Pensions would simply be a way of achieving a tax deferral on a portion of wages. Most private employment arrangements, however, do not allow for immediate vesting of pension claims in defined benefit plans. This fact alone, given competitive labor markets, undermines the usefulness of the pure deferred wage theory of pensions.

There is sound economic rationale for eligibility and vesting requirements only if pensions are contingent claims given to employees, in part as deferred wages to take advantage of the tax deferral privilege and in part as incentives to reduce labor mobility,[3] to keep employee

---

[2] Robert C. Pozen, "The Prudent Man Rule and ERISA," *Financial Analysts Journal*, vol. 33 (March/April 1977), pp. 30 ff.; and A. Gary Klesch, "Interpreting the Prudent Man Rule under ERISA," *Financial Analysts Journal*, vol. 33 (January/February), pp. 26 ff.

[3] A 1965 seven-city survey of establishments with fifty or more employees found that in the aggregate for most age groups and for most industries, the number of annual quits per 100 employees was lower in establishments with pension plans. Another study, a longitudinal survey of male workers aged forty-five to fifty-nine, found that between 1966 and 1967, 13.0 percent of all whites not eligible for pen-

monitoring costs relatively low, and to spread mortality and investment risks. The contingent claim can be exercised only upon satisfactory completion of specified service requirements and is valueless to the employee if he leaves or is fired prior to that date. Employees, too, must see merit in these requirements or they would not let them be part of the employment contract.

The Effects of ERISA. The Bankers' Trust Company surveyed a number of pension plans to determine the extent of the influence of ERISA's mandated eligibility and vesting requirements.[4] Ninety-nine firms employing more than 2 million workers responded to the survey. Twenty-eight of the plans surveyed had eligibility requirements more stringent than those permitted by ERISA and must change them to comply with the legislation.

Concerning vesting, the survey received ninety-seven usable responses. Of these firms, ninety-three now use straight ten-year vesting. The remaining four plans use graduated vesting with one plan granting full vesting within ten years, another after twelve years, and the rest after fifteen. None of the plans use the rule of forty-five. Moreover, of the ninety-seven firms, only two have vesting provisions more liberal than the ERISA requirement. Prior to ERISA, thirty-seven plans offered full vesting after ten years of service and eleven plans used a fifteen-year period. Forty-nine plans had more restrictive vesting requirements than are now allowed under ERISA. Thus, ERISA presents a binding constraint on the behavior of these firms.

Previously, firms could start counting time until vesting from a range of dates; under ERISA all employment must be counted from the time the employee is twenty-two years old. Twenty-one percent of responding firms had to change their method for crediting service for vesting as a result of ERISA.

Finally, prior to ERISA only 74 percent of the respondent firms offered preretirement death benefits to employees' spouses. As a result of this requirement, 26 percent of the firms surveyed had to adjust their pension arrangements to comply with ERISA.

In all these respects ERISA has affected the behavior of a significant number of firms.

Costs. Changes in pension provisions do not come cheaply. More liberal eligibility and vesting requirements mean that, other things

---

sion benefits changed employers, compared with only 8.4 percent of those who were eligible. See Taggart, "Labor Market Impacts of the Private Pension System," pp. 67–70.

[4] Bankers' Trust Company, *ERISA Related Changes in Corporate Pension Plans* (New York, 1976).

being equal, pension costs will rise as more employees gain pension rights. According to Morgan Guaranty Trust Company:

> Complying with the eligibility and vesting requirements typically is adding only about 1% to 3% to pension costs for companies with the most mature plans. For "median" plans the additional cost also is moderate, frequently estimated at 5% to 10%, but in some cases estimates run as high as 40%. The higher cost increases typically are found in industries such as retailing which have a high proportion of part-time employees who now have to be included in pension plans if they work as little as 1,000 hours a year, and in multi-employer plans which as a rule have had less liberal vesting provisions than single-employer plans.[5]

The adjective "only" applied to the 1 to 3 percent figures and the term "moderate" used in connection with the 5 to 10 percent estimate are obviously value judgments. More important, the dollar magnitudes involved can be significant. A 5 percent increase in costs, for example, could be enough to upset the equilibrium between the benefits derived by the corporation from a pension plan and its costs. This will naturally have negative implications for the future growth of pension benefits and of employee coverage by the private pension system.

Though the new eligibility and vesting requirements represent only a portion of the additional costs of maintaining and administering a private pension arrangement, they are not negligible. Furthermore, a reasonable fraction of any increase in the rate of terminations of old pension plans or of any decrease in the rate at which new pension plans are started should be attributable to ERISA's eligibility and vesting requirements.

Plan Terminations. Before ERISA took effect in 1975, the Pension Benefit Guaranty Corporation estimated that between 3,732 and 4,107 pension plans would terminate, about 1,000 to 2,000 of them because of ERISA. This total is considerably higher than previous experience suggested—2,577 pension plans terminated in 1974 and only 602 in 1967—but the estimate certainly seemed justified given the increased cost of operating a plan under ERISA. As it turned out, between January 1, 1975, and May 3, 1976, more than 7,600 pension plans were scrapped, with more than 5,000 of them in 1975. In addition, only 30,039 new plans were started in 1975, whereas in 1974, 59,385 new plans were initiated. From 1950 to 1975 the number of pension plans

---

[5] "Pension Plans: Adapting to ERISA," *The Morgan Guaranty Survey*, October 1976, p. 7.

rose from 12,790 to 445,397, and the drop in 1975 was only the third time the number of new plans fell below the number started the previous year.[6] ERISA appears to have prompted a dramatic change in corporate thinking about pension plans.

Though ERISA cannot be held entirely accountable for these occurrences, it is certainly somewhat responsible. Similarly, the eligibility and vesting provisions are not the only binding constraints, but they surely played an important role in slowing the growth in coverage and accelerating the rate of terminations of private pension plans.

If pensions are to create work incentives, eligibility and vesting requirements are important. If these requirements are too liberal, then no incentive effect is achieved. Since ERISA forced many firms to liberalize these requirements, one would expect the costs to these firms of providing pension plans now to exceed the benefits. And because ERISA was based on an erroneous theory of pure deferred wages, one would expect a reduced role for private pension plans in the future. If firms are compelled to move nearer the view that pension plans are merely deferred wages, they will tend to set up pension arrangements accordingly. But for many firms, the cost and complexity of administering a pure deferred wage pension program may be too great and the benefits too few.

There is, however, another side to the story. Many firms that terminated their plans very likely would not have been able to meet their pension fund promises. Similarly, many terminations were accompanied by switches to profit-sharing plans. To the extent that the law prevented outright fraud against future retirees it should be applauded. For such fraud to be perpetrated, however, employees would have to be completely misled and have no incentive to investigate the likelihood of pension promises' being kept. I am not sure that such naiveté exists in the labor market; certainly a plausible case could be made that employees do have realistic expectations of pension benefits. Moreover, in many instances, it is very likely that viable pension plans were eliminated because of the high cost of complying with ERISA.

Financial Aspects

Prior to ERISA, firms were required to make annual contributions large enough to cover benefits currently earned by participants. They did not have any special requirements to fund benefits that arose as a

---

[6] Robert D. Paul, "The Impact of Pension Reform on American Business," *Sloan Management Review*, vol. 18, no. 1 (Fall 1976), pp. 61–62.

result of liberalizing benefits on past service, although they were obliged to pay interest on the unfunded portion. These past service liabilities must now be funded over a period of forty years. For new firms or for future changes in benefit levels, funding must take place over a thirty-year period. Initially, this requirement seemed to be not particularly onerous, and recent theoretical work has shown that in the absence of taxes, funding policy is largely irrelevant to the market value of the firm when the pension debt and the marketable debt are similar in status. In this sense, an unfunded pension fund liability is analogous to an issue of marketable securities.[7] The pension fund debt is not identical to regular debt, however. It was, prior to ERISA, unsecured; its priority status in liquidation was below that of secured debt; and its tax implications are different from those of regular debt. Ironically, most firms have some amount of pension fund debt, and this is difficult to explain in light of the analysis by Tepper and Affleck.[8] They showed that by issuing marketable debt in order to fund pensions, a firm could gain a net tax advantage since both the pension fund contribution and the interest on the debt would be tax deductible. With only pension fund debt, a deductible expense would be forgone. Available analyses therefore seem to indicate that pension funding is irrelevant or that selling regular debt is the preferable way to fund pensions. Such analyses suggest that ERISA's funding rules either should make no difference to corporate equity valuation or may actually benefit shareholders. These analyses are not without flaw. Funding policy may be quite relevant, as may be seen by examining why firms are not now taking advantage of the tax benefits.

Pension Fund Debt and Equity Valuation. One frequently mentioned reason firms are not now taking advantage of tax benefits is that unfunded pension fund liabilities have the advantage of "off-balance sheet" financing. If the securities markets do not recognize the existence of these liabilities in valuing the equity of a firm, the equity value would be higher than otherwise and the true amount of debt would be understated. This reasoning is fallacious, however, in the context of an efficient securities market that correctly incorporates all economically relevant information in the prices of assets. Moreover, under current standards, these financial data are being reported. Oldfield supports the view that markets are efficient, and he concludes that

---

[7] See Sharpe, "Corporate Pension Funding Policy."

[8] I. Tepper and A. R. P. Affleck, "Pension Plan Liabilities and Corporate Financial Policies," *Journal of Finance*, vol. 29 (December 1974), pp. 1549–1564.

corporate equity valuation reflects unfunded pension fund liabilities.[9] His empirical study is the only one that explicitly treats this issue and and is based on recent data.

An alternative view of why firms did not fully fund past service liabilities focuses on the priority of the various debt claims. Pre-ERISA, pension fund liabilities had low status. A senior creditor could therefore feel reasonably secure about the value of his claim; corporate managers, by virtue of their own pension claims, had an interest in making decisions that would allow the firm to fund past service obligations, that is, to meet the pension fund liability as it came due. If these obligations were met, all senior debt would, of course, be serviced.[10] In addition, the firm may have been able to issue liabilities to its pension fund with less onerous indenture provisions than the marketable securities it would have had to sell to fund the pension liability directly. If the equity value to the firm of avoiding onerous bond covenants or indenture provisions exceeded the value of the net tax advantage of funding through a marketable issue, then the policies pursued by firms were economically sensible. Similarly, if the value to unsecured debt holders of having junior debt in the form of pension fund liabilities exceeded the net tax advantage to the equity holders, and if the interest paid on marketable unsecured debt was less with than that without junior unfunded pension liabilities and the difference was more than the tax advantage, then unfunded liabilities were economically sensible. In addition, the firm could economize on the transactions costs associated with public issues by issuing pension fund debt rather than marketable debt. Regardless of the specifics of the situation, firms could choose from an array of funding options and funding schedules. Because of changes in accounting standards, the array was not as wide as it might have been, but there was more flexibility than there is now. Even though ERISA's requirements seem relatively innocuous, they may have an adverse affect on the equity value of the firm and on the interest rates that must be paid on marketable debt. This is independent of the change in the priority structure of debt required by ERISA.

Debt Priority. In addition to eliminating certain funding policies, ERISA alters the priority of the firm's past service obligations to the

---

[9] Oldfield, "Financial Aspects of the Private Pension System."

[10] This is analogous to the agency arguments advanced in Jensen and Meckling, "Theory of the Firm: Managerial Behavior, Agency Costs, and Ownership Structure."

71

pension fund. Up to a defined limit, these obligations to the pension fund now have the status of federal tax liens, that is, they have priority over all other forms of corporate debt except workers' unpaid wages. ERISA has recontracted with the regular debt holders, the employees, and the shareholders. By altering the property rights of the owners of financial assets, it may have contributed to the poor performance of equity markets in recent years.

The PBGC. ERISA establishes a quasi-governmental agency, the Pension Benefit Guaranty Corporation, to deal with pension fund terminations. If a plan is terminated with insufficient funds to meet promised pension benefits, the PBGC pays vested benefits up to $750 per month, adjusted for future changes in the social security system's tax base.[11] These insured benefits are financed by annual premiums paid by the pension funds. In addition, a pension fund that PBGC deems inadequately funded can be forced to terminate, and PBGC will assume responsibility for paying benefits, claiming up to 30 percent of the firm's net worth as reimbursement. Firms can privately insure against this claim on their net worth, although it may be some time before such insurance is available from either commercial insurers or the PBGC itself. At present the PBGC is still struggling with how this might work, and there is a chance that this provision of the law will be repealed.

The law provides that the insurance coverage provided by the PBGC will take effect only after premiums have been paid for five years. There has been no rush by private insurers to offer coverage, let alone coverage which takes effect prior to the PBGC's. The firm's equity holders have been exposed to additional risk by the law's provision for involuntary termination, and the rights of the firm's debt holders have been diminished by the reduction in the status of their claims.

Magnitudes. Table 22 shows unfunded vested benefits as a percentage of net worth, unfunded past service costs as a percentage of net worth, and the combination of these two for a forty-firm sample. It also shows the ratio of regular debt to equity after the value of stockholders' equity has been adjusted to reflect the unfunded pension claim. This adjustment was limited to 30 percent of net worth in keeping with the limits of the liability. Although the data do not take account of

---

[11] The increases in the tax base in the 1977 amendments are very large and were probably unanticipated. This could lead to a reconsideration of the relationship between PBGC benefits and the tax base.

TABLE 22

1975 FINANCIAL DATA ON PENSION FUND DEBT AND REGULAR DEBT

Company	Unfunded Vested Benefits as Percent of Net Worth	Unfunded Past Service Costs as Percent of Net Worth	Total Pension Fund Debt as Percent of Net Worth	Regular Long-Term Debt as Percent of Stockholders Equity[a]
General Motors	22	51	73	9
Ford	16	46	62	24
Chrysler	48	79	127	44
American Motors	42	78	120	36
DuPont	6	17	33	23
Union Carbide	5	22	27	46
Monsanto	3	17	20	43
Dow Chemical	2	N.A.	N.A.	64
Warner-Lambert	0	8	8	24
Johnson & Johnson	0	N.A.	N.A.	3
American Home Products	0	0	0	0
Pfizer	0	3	3	51
General Electric	11	14	25	26
Westinghouse	25	31	56	30
Combustion Engineering	7	24	31	27
Babcock & Wilcox	25	38	63	46
Beatrice Foods	0.3	6	6	27
Kraftco	1	3	4	23
General Foods	0	N.A.	N.A.	24
Borden	5	11	16	39
Eastman Kodak	0	0	0	2
Caterpillar Tractor	25	54	79	48
Lockheed	437	N.A.	N.A.	1080
Western Union	42	49	91	116
IBM	0	3	3	3
Xerox	0	0	0	59
Sperry Rand	0	N.A.	N.A.	44
Honeywell	0	13	13	49
Sears	2	5	7	25
J. C. Penney	0	3	3	22
Kresge	0	N.A.	N.A.	18
F. W. Woolworth	5	1	6	48

(Table continues on next page.)

Table 22 (Continued)

Company	Unfunded Vested Benefits as Percent of Net Worth	Unfunded Past Service Costs as Percent of Net Worth	Total Pension Fund Debt as Percent of Net Worth	Regular Long-Term Debt as Percent of Stock-holders Equity[a]
U.S. Steel	6	25	31	32
Bethlehem Steel	50	44	94	33
Armco Steel	15	53	68	33
Republic Steel	34	60	94	28
Goodyear	19	24	43	48
Firestone	8	25	33	47
Universal	82	94	176	74
B. F. Goodrich	22	42	64	60

N.A.: Not available.

[a] Adjusted for pension claims, but in no case by more than 30 percent.

Source: Patrick J. Regan, *The 1976 BEA Pension Survey* (New York: BEA Associates, July 1976).

the fact that leases have very likely not been capitalized and the debt of captive finance companies is excluded, they do show that there is a good deal of money at stake.

Most firms in this sample have substantial unfunded liabilities. Moreover, their debt to equity ratios are considerably greater than they would be otherwise because of contingent claims on unfunded pensions. This indicates that ERISA has increased the financial risk of the firm and may already have affected equity values adversely.

Bankruptcy. Unlike stockholders, senior debt holders may find the PBGC helpful despite the seniority of its claim. In principle, the PBGC can force termination of the plan and perhaps force liquidation of the firm before conventional bankruptcy is reached, thus potentially helping senior debt holders achieve a higher return than they otherwise would.[12]

But senior debt holders should not rely on this possibility, because the PBGC is not adequately equipped to monitor firms closely. For

---

[12] For a full treatment of this issue and the question of the effect of ERISA on equity holders, see Treynor, Regan, and Priest, *Financial Realities of Pension Funding under ERISA.*

junior debt holders, too, this possibility may not be important, because their claims may be so subordinate that they would prefer to keep the firm operational in hopes of its making a comeback. Both classes of holders might still prefer the pre-ERISA low priority pension fund debt arrangement that gave management and employees a stronger interest in meeting all debt obligations because their own claims were near the bottom of the list.

Equity Holders. Shareholders derive no benefit from the ERISA provisions of contingent claims on the firm, insurance of pension plans, or the PBGC's right to terminate plans. If the pension claims were both fully insured and fully funded, and if the variability of the value of pension fund assets were small, shareholders would be only negligibly affected by ERISA. Shareholders may suffer, however, because they bear the risk associated with fluctuations in the value of the pension fund assets. And if ERISA's provisions concerning fiduciary responsibility prevent pension funds from investing in securities with high expected returns because of the risks, pension funding costs would rise and, without corresponding product price increases, corporate earnings would decline. Also, the PBGC may have the authority to limit dividends to shareholders, depending upon the interpretation of section 4062 of the act.

Financial Contracts. ERISA has altered a whole range of freely contracted financial arrangements. Treynor, Regan, and Priest argue that "ERISA can be regarded as confiscatory only if companies had no intention of honoring their pension promises to employees."[13] However, to the extent that ERISA precludes portfolio returns which are higher than those that can be achieved with legally "safe" investments, it is confiscatory. It leads to a rise in pension costs, in relation to benefits, at the expense of equity holders of the corporation.

More important, the new requirements and fiduciary guidelines have not been worked out, and much testing is expected through litigation and additional legislation. The uncertainty facing firms has been increased substantially by the passage of the act. One would expect the growth in pension fund coverage to slow rather dramatically and the rate of voluntary plan terminations to increase.

Benefits and Costs

ERISA has reduced uncertainty about private retirement benefits and has to some extent standardized pension contracts. But ultimately its

---

13 Ibid., p. 88.

most significant feature may be the possibility of tax deferral on retirement savings through IRAs. ERISA has also mandated rules for eligibility and vesting, altered financial arrangements among stockholders, bondholders, and pension claimants, and dictated change in many of the financial policies of firms. The imposition of such binding constraints cannot possibly make all the affected parties better off than they were before. Sorting these parties out, however, is no simple task—who wins and who loses depends on the starting position of each firm's pension arrangements and the financial condition of each firm's pension funds.

Winners and Losers. Firms which already had liberal pension provisions, fully funded plans, and pension funds invested in very low-risk assets will neither gain nor lose. But a substantial number of firms were not in this situation.

If eligibility and vesting provisions were formerly more stringent than those required by ERISA, the newly qualified employees gain, except to the extent that firms reduce their pension benefits to compensate for the greater number of those who qualify. If benefits are reduced, long-time employees would lose. If benefits cannot be reduced, shareholders would suffer because of the change in the compensation requirements and because the reduction in incentives might require high expenditures on monitoring and supervising employees.

As a result of ERISA's eligibility and vesting provisions, many firms may find it uneconomic to offer pension plans. Employees of terminated plans would suffer if the termination payment had a lower present value than the full pension payment. Similarly, employees of firms which decide against offering pension plans may lose some benefits associated with tax deferral on a portion of their compensation if the amount that would be set aside through a pension plan exceeded the amount that can be set aside through an individual retirement account. Shareholders who viewed pension plans as incentive contracts would lose in the event of termination or non-starting of pension plans, for they must develop alternative, presumably less beneficial arrangements to achieve the same results.

Under the new funding provisions and other financial policies, covered workers gain because the probability of pension fund insolvency has been lessened. However, uncovered but potentially covered workers may lose if the new rules make it too difficult for a firm to initiate a plan. IRAs can now be substituted for pensions by these workers, but the amount of savings that can be set aside may be less than the amount that the firm would have set aside. To some workers, a risky pension fund might be more attractive than no corporate pension plan.

Until it is known how the courts interpret ERISA and how Congress may modify it, the effect of its financial provisions on shareholders is difficult to predict beyond the prospect of increased risks owing to contingent claims and the increased costs related to employee incentives. Because the increases in risk and cost come about without apparent corresponding shareholder benefits, shareholders are likely to lose. Perhaps a portion of the recent poor performance of security markets could be attributed to the uncompensated transfer of property rights from shareholders.

6

Social Security and Corporate Pension Plans

One of the objectives of ERISA was to lessen future demands on the social security system by "strengthening" the private pension system.[1] It was expected that so long as corporate pension programs were economically healthy, those collecting private pension benefits would not insist on larger social security benefits. But ERISA may in fact reduce the attractiveness of private pension plans to employers, slowing the growth in private pensions or perhaps reducing the number of firms offering them and the number of workers covered by them. Recent changes in the social security system also have weakened the private pension system and will probably increase rather than decrease future demands on social security.

This chapter discusses the technical aspects of the integration of private pension plans with social security and then presents data on the different types of integration. It also explores the effect of integration on private pension payments. Corporate problems arise from the possibility that legislation will change the way benefits may be integrated, and from the negative influence of social security benefits on the incentive effects of private pensions. The chapter concludes with a discussion of some broader issues raised by the social security program and its interaction with private pension plans.

Integration of Social Security and Private Pension Plans

Why and How. In terms of replacement rates (the ratio of retirement income to final pay), the benefits from private pensions and social security are negatively related when the two types of plans are integrated. The adjustment takes place in·the private component. The

---

[1] For a recent study of the social security system, see Munnell, *The Future of Social Security*.

intent of integration is the maintenance of roughly constant replacement ratios across employee income groups. Low-income earners obtain a comparatively high replacement ratio from their social security benefits (see Tables 28–32) and smaller replacement from private plans. High-income earners, on the other hand, achieve comparatively low replacement from social security because of the Primary Insurance Amount (PIA) benefit formula and relatively high replacement from private plans.

Raymond Schmitt describes the concept of integration:

> The Internal Revenue Code permits private pension plans to integrate their benefit formulas with benefits provided under Social Security. . . . Social Security laws set a ceiling on the amount of wages subject to payroll tax. Since Social Security benefits are related to covered earnings they also have a built-in ceiling. Thus, Social Security income replacement rates decrease as preretirement income increases. It was considered logical, therefore, to permit the private pension system to pick up where the Social Security system left off by providing supplemental benefits based upon earnings above the Social Security wage base.
>
> Congress recognized this in 1942, when it first wrote into the law the proviso that although a tax qualified plan could not discriminate in favor of the higher paid workers its benefit structure could favor those with earnings above the Social Security ceiling provided that when the public and private benefits were considered together, their combined benefits did not give preference to the higher paid. So long as the ratio of combined benefits to earnings is no higher for employees whose wages exceed the taxable wage base than for those whose wages are fully taxed by Social Security, Congress said a plan would be held to be nondiscriminatory.
>
> A ruling by the Internal Revenue Service implements this nondiscrimination requirement by specifying certain limits to benefits (or contributions) that a private pension plan must observe in order for the plan to receive special tax treatment. These limits govern the extent to which retirement benefits based on earnings above the Social Security taxable wage base can exceed benefits based on earnings below it.[2]

The defined contribution plan is typically integrated with social security by reducing the employer's contribution to the private plan.

---

[2] Raymond Schmitt, "Integration of Private Pension Plans with Social Security," in Subcommittee on Fiscal Policy of the Joint Economic Committee, 93rd Congress, 2nd session, *Issues in Financing Retirement Income*, Studies in Public Welfare, Paper no. 18 (Washington, D.C., 1974), p. 175.

TABLE 23

OFFSET METHOD OF INTEGRATING DEFINED BENEFIT PLAN WITH SOCIAL SECURITY

Compen-sation Base[a] (dollars)	Monthly Benefits[b] (dollars)			Total Replace-ment Ratio
	Social security	Private pension	Total	
500	260.00	0.00	260.00	0.52
1,000	360.00	270.00	630.00	0.63
2,000	387.00	706.50	1,093.50	0.55

[a] Average monthly earnings for last three years of work.
[b] Of three employees with different earnings, each retiring in 1975 after thirty years' service.

Suppose that an employer contributes x percent of an employee's salary to social security and the private pension plan combined. If the employer's share of the social security contribution is less than x percent of the employee's salary, the difference goes to the private pension plan.

There are two broad methods of integrating defined benefit plans: the offset approach and the excess approach. In the offset approach, the defined benefit is first computed according to the prevailing formula (years of service multiplied by the compensation base multiplied by some percentage). From that product is subtracted a percentage of the social security benefit (typically 50 percent, but in some cases up to 83.33 percent). The private pension benefit is the remainder; if the remainder is zero or negative, there is no private benefit unless the firm has established a minimum pension.

Consider the case of three employees with different average monthly earnings for the last three years of work, retiring in 1975, each with thirty years' service. Their monthly benefits can be computed under the offset method with the following formula (see Table 23):

1.5 percent × number of years worked × average monthly salary for last three years − 50 percent of social security benefit.

Although the offset approach discriminates against the low-wage worker with respect to private pension benefits, the total replacement

TABLE 24

Compen-sation Base[a] (dollars)	Social Security Replace-ment Ratio[b]	Excess Plan		Step-Rate Excess Plan	
		Private benefit[c] (dollars)	Private replace-ment ratio	Private benefit[c]	Private replace-ment ratio
500	0.52	30.00	0.06	126.00	0.25
1,000	0.36	180.00	0.18	276.00	0.27
2,000	0.19	460.00	0.23	576.00	0.28

[a] Average monthly earnings for last three years of work.

[b] Based on data in Table 23.

[c] Monthly private pension benefit of three employees with different earnings, each retiring in 1975 after thirty years' service.

ratio is approximately as large as that of high-wage earners because of integration with social security.

The excess method of social security integration also allows for different private pension benefits on different levels of income. An excess plan pays private benefits on earnings above a stipulated level, and no benefits, or benefits at some lower rate, on earnings below that stipulated level. When benefits are paid on earnings below the stipulated level, the plan is referred to as a "step-rate" excess plan.[3] The following examples are typical pension formulas under these plans:

Excess: 1.0 percent × number of years worked × (monthly compensation base − $400).

Step-rate excess: 1.0 percent × number of years worked × (monthly compensation base − $400) + 0.8 percent × number of years of service × $400.

These formulas can be used to figure private pension replacement for three employees with different earnings, each with thirty years of service (see Table 24). For workers with low earnings, social security payments make up for the lower private pension benefits. The results in Table 24 are affected by the particular percentages used and the "excess" breakpoint. Firms can choose an excess breakpoint up to the

[3] For elaboration of these and other methods which are similar to the excess approach described, see ibid.

TABLE 25

Limits to Social Security Integration with Private Plans

Year of IRS Ruling	Maximum Wage Base in Excess Plans (dollars)	Maximum Differential in Step-Rate Excess Approach (percent)	Maximum Social Security Offset (percent of difference)	Social Security Benefits Attributed to Employer Contribution (percent)
1943	3,000	25.00	150.00	100.00
1951	3,600	37.50	140.00	93.75
1953	3,600	37.50	130.00	87.50
1956	4,200	37.50	120.00	80.00
1961	4,800	37.50	117.00	78.00
1967	6,600	27.25	85.00	78.00
1969	7,800	30.00	75.00	50.00
1971	9,000	37.50	83.33	50.00

Source: Raymond Schmitt, "Integration of Private Pension Plans with Social Security," in Subcommittee on Fiscal Policy of the Joint Economic Committee, 93rd Congress, 2nd Session, *Issues in Financing Retirement Income*, Studies in Public Welfare, Paper no. 18 (Washington, D.C., 1974), appendix 4, p. 196.

maximum social security wage base. The larger the wage base, the less the private plan must pay, other things being equal.

Table 25 shows the changes in the limitations on integration set by the Internal Revenue Service from 1943 to 1971.[4] The assumptions made in arriving at the allowable maximums appear to be relatively arbitrary and closely parallel the opinions of the IRS authorities concerning the portion of the social security tax borne by the employer. These change over time, and while the offset percentage has decreased, the percentage difference in the step-rate approach has not been altered dramatically. The rise in the maximum wage base conforms to the social security tax base.

If pensions are integrated with social security, increases in real social security benefits lead to a reduction in the contractual private obligations of firms. This is not consistent with the deferred wage theory of pensions. The deferred wage theory implies that the wealth held for the employee in the pension fund actually belongs to the employee after he or she achieves vested status. In an integrated plan,

---

[4] For more detail on the Internal Revenue Service limits and discussion of how these estimates were made, see ibid., pp. 193–198.

however, an employee's pension wealth changes with every change in the social security law—in effect, the private plan is recontracted. If accumulated pension wealth is viewed as the compound value of deferred wages, an exogenous event should not reduce it. Consider the example of the $1,000 per month employee in Table 23. If on the day before retirement his social security benefits jumped to $900, he could be entitled to no private pension. The social security system would provide his retirement income, and the firm would not have to fulfill its direct pension obligation. If pensions were nothing more than deferred wages, no justification exists for denying the employee his share in the pension fund. On the other hand, if pensions are viewed as incentive arrangements, the employee's rights would not be violated. The firm would keep its promise of providing retirement income in old age. It would treat the contingent claim of the employee as one against income—with the firm bearing the risk of no changes in social security benefits—rather than as a right to accumulated wealth (a share of the pension fund asset) or a deferred wage. Although integration with social security violates the pure deferred wage concept, but not the contingent claim notion of pensions, pensions based on the contingent claim view need not be integrated; there may still exist a rationale for additional incentives through additive private pensions.

The Extent of Integration. The most comprehensive survey of integration has been made by Schmitt.[5] His findings are based on a sample of 369 large plans (more than twenty-six employees) and 425 small plans (less than twenty-six employees) and are believed to be representative of approximately 412,300 corporate pension, profit-sharing, and stock bonus plans. He found that: (1) Sixty percent of the plans have some type of integration with social security. (2) Only 25 to 30 percent of the workers covered by private pension plans are in integrated plans, and small plans have a higher incidence of integration than large plans. (3) Integrated plans typically affect salaried employees rather than hourly employees, and they affect conventional plans to a far greater extent than pattern plans. Schmitt's third finding is similar to the findings based on the data from the Bankers' Trust. However, his findings concerning the higher incidence of integration in small plans than in large plans and the relatively small portion of covered workers may be misleading.

Table 26 shows the types of social security integration, by type of formula, in a sample of 190 plans surveyed by Bankers' Trust. Among final pay plans, offset formulas are the most popular, whereas among

---

[5] Ibid., p. 174.

TABLE 26

Types of Social Security Integration in Conventional
Pension Plans, by Type of Formula, 1970 and 1975

(percent)

	1975	1970
Final Pay Formulas		
Offset	52	50
Step-up	34	38
Excess	1	1
Nonintegrated	13	11
Total	100	100
Career average formulas		
Offset	3	3
Step-up	81	85
Excess	3	3
Nonintegrated	13	9
Total	100	100

Source: Bankers' Trust Company, *Study of Corporate Pension Plans*, various issues.

career average plans, most use the step-up excess approach. For both
types of plans, there is a small decline in the number of firms that are
integrated. In 1975, 13 percent of final pay plans did not integrate,
compared with 11 percent in 1970; for career average plans, the percentage of plans that were nonintegrated rose from 9 to 13 percent
from 1970 to 1975.

In addition to the decline in the percentage of firms integrating
their plans, the magnitude of integration also declined from 1970 to
1975.[6] With respect to offset plans, 12 percent of the sample firms
reduced the private benefit by more than 50 percent of the primary
social security benefit in 1975, whereas in 1970, 43 percent of the
sample firms used offset percentages of more than 50 percent. In 1975,
65 percent used offsets of 50 percent, compared with 45 percent that
chose 50 percent offsets in 1970. Similarly, in 1975 two out of three
firms using an offset approach graduated the offset by length of service.
For an employee reaching retirement age prior to the maximum period
for offset, the offset percentage will be lower. With a maximum serv-

[6] Bankers' Trust Company, *1975 Study of Corporate Pension Plans*, p. 28.

ice of forty years and a 50 percent social security offset, a worker retiring after thirty years of service may face an offset of only 40 percent. In 1970, only one of every three firms using the offset method of integration used a graduated approach.

With respect to the breakpoint used in excess and step-rate excess methods, rather than specifying dollar amounts, firms are indexing to the social security wage base. In 1970, four out of five excess plans indicated specific dollar amounts; in 1975 less than three in five did so. The remaining two in five set the breakpoint as a fraction of the social security tax base.

In general, over the past several years there has been a slight reduction in the incidence and stringency of social security integration. This would push up private benefits if computation formulas remained the same. But other changes have kept private benefits from rising more than final salaries, and total replacement ratios have not changed by any appreciable amount (see Table 10).

The Wyatt Company's survey of industrial retirement plans provides additional information about the incidence and magnitude of social security integration, for a small sample of large firms (see Table 27). Of the fifty largest U.S. industrial firms (utilities excluded), forty-eight offer pension plans of some kind; the other two (Proctor and Gamble and Xerox) have profit-sharing plans. Forty-three of these plans integrate a portion of their benefits (including minimum pension) in some way with social security benefits. Twenty-six plans use an offset approach in some instances, and for twenty-one the maximum offset is 50 percent of the primary social security benefit. Twenty-three use some type of excess approach. A few of the plans use both methods in various ways such as in alternative computations of benefits, in arriving at a minimum pension benefit, or in determining the employee's contribution to the plan. Although this finding that social security integration has been widely adopted conflicts with the studies by Schmitt, it is consistent with the surveys by the Bankers' Trust. While the Bankers' Trust and Wyatt sample firms may be unrepresentative because of their large size and sophistication, they are trend-setters. These firms are the nation's largest employers, and their policies toward integration are very significant.

Table 27 shows the important features of each of the forty-eight pension plans in the Wyatt survey. In the first column, maximum social security offset, the symbol "G" indicates that the offset is graduated by years of service. A few plans are entered in both the offset and excess columns because alternative computations may be used to determine benefits. Since the completion of the survey, some of the firms may have altered their plans. Also, because these plans cover

TABLE 27

SOCIAL SECURITY INTEGRATION POLICIES IN THE FORTY-EIGHT LARGEST U.S. INDUSTRIAL CORPORATONS WITH PENSION PLANS, JULY 1, 1975

Firm	Maximum Social Security Offset (percent)	Excess	Minimum Pension	Employee Contribution
Amerada Hess	50%, G	—	—	—
Armco Steel	65%	—	—	—
Ashland Oil	—	1.5% of $1,000 over career average 2.25% of excess 1% of $750 over final pay 1.5% of excess	—	3% of excess over $1,000
Atlantic Richfield	—	1.15% of social security tax base 1.5% of excess	—	—
Beatrice Foods	50%, G	—	—	—
Bethlehem Steel	50%	—	—	—
Boeing	50%	—	—	—
Borden	—	*Noncontributory* 1.5% of excess over social security tax base *Contributory* 1% of excess over social security tax base	—	5% of excess over social security tax base

Company			*Offset*	
Caterpillar Tractor	—		—	—
Chrysler	—		60% of social security tax base	2.5% of excess over ⅔ social security tax base
Continental Oil	50%, G		—	—
Dow Chemical	50%, G		—	—
DuPont	50%		—	—
Eastman Kodak	—	1.2% of average social security tax base 1.4% of excess	—	—
Esmark	50%		—	—
Exxon	50%, G		—	—
Firestone	50%, G (final pay)	1.3% of $900 over career average 2% of excess	—	3.5% of excess over $900
Ford	—	2% of excess over ⅔ social security tax base	—	3.5% above ⅔ of the social security tax base (subject to maximum)
General Electric	—	1% of $550 2.1% of excess	—	3% of excess over $550
General Motors	—	1.5% of excess over $500 1.0% of excess over $1,150 for final five years	—	3% of excess over $500

(*Table continues on next page.*)

TABLE 27 (Continued)

Firm	Maximum Social Security Offset (percent)	Excess	Minimum Pension	Employee Contribution
Goodyear Tire and Rubber	—	1.75% of earnings in excess of monthly base amount (unspecified)	—	3.5% of excess over $1,050 until age 55 then 4% above $1,050
W. R. Grace	50%	—	—	—
Greyhound	—	—	—	—
Gulf Oil	50%, G	—	—	—
IBM	—	1% of $400 1.5% of excess	—	—
International Harvester	—	2% of excess over social security tax base	55% of highest year less social security benefit	6% of excess over social security tax base
ITT	50%, G	—	—	—
Kraftco	—	1% of $300–$600 2% of excess 0.667% of average earnings over $400 for final ten years	50% of social security benefit	3% of $300–$600 6% of excess
Lockheed Aircraft	—	1.5% of excess over $350	—	—

LTV Corp.	50%, G	—	—	—
Mobil Oil	50%, G	—	—	—
Monsanto	—	1.5% of excess over social security tax base 1.1% of social security tax base 0.75% of excess over social security tax base, final five years	—	4.5% of excess over social security tax base
Occidental Petroleum	—	—	—	—
Phillips Petroleum	50%, G (final pay)	1.3% of social security tax base 1.75% of excess over career average	Benefit reduced by social security benefit	—
RCA	—	1.125% of $550 2% of excess	—	3% of excess over $550
R. J. Reynolds Industries	—	1.25% of $650 1.5% of excess	—	—
Rockwell International	—	1.5% of excess over $566.67	—	—
Shell Oil	50%, G	—	—	—
Standard Oil of California	37.5%, G	—	—	—
Standard Oil of Indiana	50%, G (final pay)	1.5% of social security tax base 2% of excess over career average	—	—

(Table continues on next page.)

TABLE 27 (Continued)

Firm	Maximum Social Security Offset (percent)	Excess	Minimum Pension	Employee Contribution
Sun Oil	50%, G	—	—	—
Tenneco	—	1.375% of $350 2.25% of excess	—	—
Texaco	45%, G (final pay)	1.31% of $650 2% of excess over career average	—	0.655% of $650 1% of excess
Union Carbide	—	—	—	—
Union Oil of California	50%, G	—	—	—
U.S. Steel	—	—	—	—
United Technologies	—	1.5% of $1,175 2.25% of excess	50% of social security benefit	2% of excess over $1,175
Westinghouse Electric	—	2.1% of excess over $550	—	2.5% of excess over $550

Dash (—): Not applicable.

G: Indicates the offset is graduated by years of service.

SOURCE: Wyatt Company, *Survey of Retirement, Thrift and Profit Sharing Plans Covering Salaried Employees of the 50 Largest U.S. Industrial Companies*, Washington, D.C., July 1, 1975.

only salaried employees, they may not provide a totally accurate picture of the current status of social security integration.

In the ten firms which integrate social security either through the offset or the excess method where the breakpoint meshes with social security tax bases, increases in social security benefits as well as increases in wage bases result in the lowering of private pension benefits. If social security benefits (for offset plans) and social security tax bases (for excess plans) rise faster than wages, an increasing number of employees of these firms will receive very small private benefits. Under such conditions, integration, coupled with rising real social security benefits, could undermine private pension plans. As expected private benefits decline, the incentive effects of private plans decline as well. This, in fact, could be the reason for the slight trend toward liberalized integration rules indicated by the results of the Bankers' Trust surveys.

The Effect of Integration. The advantage to firms of integration schemes is the "savings" they expect to achieve in their pension costs by integrating their formulas with social security. Schmitt explored how much it would cost firms to provide the private benefits displaced by social security. He surveyed life insurance companies managing the pension plans of small firms and asked how much private plan costs would increase if they could no longer integrate with social security but still maintained the benefit levels implied by the nonintegrated portions of their formulas. Although there are data problems and methodological difficulties with this approach to the question, he concluded that the increase in pension costs would average 58 percent if the plans were no longer integrated.[7]

Table 28 shows that a firm's pension costs could rise by nearly 50 percent if it were prevented from integrating its plan with social security—and did not scale back its plan. If all integrated plans were no longer allowed to integrate with social security, there would undoubtedly be widespread reductions in their benefit formulas. Such cutbacks would probably apply only to new workers and to the remaining portion of the careers of older workers. If legislation prohibiting integration were passed, the increase in costs to firms could be large enough to put some firms in severe financial difficulty, and some might drop their pension plans.

Table 29 shows how the private pension benefit replacement ratios of the forty-eight large firms in the Wyatt survey would change in response to the indexing of social security benefits to increases in

---

[7] Schmitt, "Integration of Private Pension Plans," p. 185.

TABLE 28

	Integrated[a]	Nonintegrated[b]
Number of active employees	563	563
Basic data summary (dollars)		
Average annual compensation	15,677	15,677
Average projected final average pay	40,003	40,003
Average projected annual pension	14,187	21,351
Basic valuation results (thousands of dollars)		
Gross accrued actuarial liability		
Active employees	6,429	8,539
Retired and vested employees	2,865	2,865
Total	9,294	11,404
Valuation assets	5,454	5,454
Net accrued actuarial liability	3,840	5,950
Annual normal cost	316	452
Illustrative annual contribution (thousands of dollars)		
Annual normal cost	316	452
Amortization of net actuarial liability over thirty years	289	448
Total annual contribution	605	900

[a] Integrated formula: (1.5 percent of final five-year average pay − 1.25 percent of social security primary insurance amount) × (years of service).

[b] Nonintegrated formula: (1.5 percent of final five-year average pay) × (years of service).

NOTE: The following assumptions are made: an interest rate of 7 percent, an annual salary increase of 4.5 percent, an annual wage base increase of 4 percent, and an annual increase in consumer price index of 3 percent.

SOURCE: Commentary by Edwin F. Boynton, in Colin D. Campbell, ed., *Financing Social Security* (Washington, D.C.: American Enterprise Institute, 1979), p. 295.

prices. It is based on 1975 data and computations made by the Wyatt Company. Column 1 shows the private pension replacement ratio for a worker retiring in 1975 at age sixty-five after thirty-five years of participation in the firm's pension plan. It is assumed that the starting salary is $5,271.04 per year and that it rises by 4 percent per year to yield a final monthly salary of $1,667.65, or annual salary of $20,012.04. The monthly social security benefit used in all offset formulas is $341.60, and excess methods vary according to specifications. Column 2 shows the private pension benefit replacement ratio for a worker retiring in 2010 at the age of sixty-five *without automatic social security increases.* Starting salary is assumed to be $15,000, and salary grows 4 percent annually. Final salary is $57,514.80 per year, or $4,742.90 per month. The monthly social security benefit is fixed at $522.80, and the taxable social security wage base is also fixed. Column 3 gives private pension replacement ratios *with automatic social security increases* for a worker retiring in 2010 at age sixty-five with thirty-five years of service. Salary assumptions are the same as for Column 2. The monthly primary social security benefit at time of retirement is assumed to grow to $2,003.40 or by 3 percent per year —the same as the cost of living. Resultant figures are used in offset formulas. The social security tax base grows at 4 percent per year. In the excess method computation, the excess is a function of the taxable wage base. With no automatic social security increases, replacement from social security is estimated to be 21 percent; with automatic increases the social security replacement ratio is 42.2 percent.

The differences between column 2 and column 3 demonstrate the power of social security integration. As social security benefits rise over the period to 2010, the replacement provided by most of the private plans in Table 29 declines. Average private replacement for all plans for a worker retiring in 1975 is 42.1 percent, and the average private replacement for a worker retiring in 2010 with no automatic social security benefit increases is 44.4 percent—similar to the current situation. For employees retiring in 2010 with automatic social security increases, however, the average private replacement declines to 35.3 percent.

For the five nonintegrated plans, average private replacement is 46.3 percent, and with automatic increases social security payments will provide an additional 42.2 percent—a total of 88.5 percent, a rather high replacement by historical standards (see Tables 28–32). Given the larger tax exemptions allowed at age sixty-five, the nontaxability of social security benefits, and the reduction in work-related expenses, employees belonging to nonintegrated plans will probably receive higher after-tax income in retirement than while working. This would not appear to trouble firms offering nonintegrated plans, because they specified the contracts and they wrote the rules for their own reasons. In fact, such high replacement ratios may pose a problem for these firms because it may induce their employees to retire sooner than age sixty-five, even when the firms would prefer to retain them.

Most of the conventional pension plans for salaried employees in the samples studied by Bankers' Trust and Wyatt are integrated with

TABLE 29

Effects of Social Security Growth on Integrated Private Pension Replacement Ratios

(percent)

Firm	Retire 1975 (1)	Retire 2010; No Automatic Social Security Increases (2)	Retire 2010; Automatic Social Security Increases (3)
Amerada Hess	38.4	43.1	27.5
Armco Steel	35.3	41.4	32.9
Ashland Oil	42.6	47.4	47.7
Atlantic Richfield	47.4	47.5	44.2
Beatrice Foods	35.1	39.9	32.4
Bethlehem Steel	38.4	43.1	29.5
Boeing	33.5	25.0	10.9
Borden	47.2	51.5	28.0
Caterpillar Tractor[a]	48.6	48.6	48.6
Chrysler	40.6	39.7	21.0
Continental Oil	43.6	48.4	32.8
Dow Chemical	39.0	39.9	24.3
DuPont	38.9	43.1	38.9
Eastman Kodak	45.4	45.4	40.9
Esmark	38.4	43.1	27.5
Exxon	43.6	48.4	32.8
Firestone	37.2	41.9	26.8
Ford	57.7	56.9	55.2
General Electric	37.7	36.3	36.3
General Motors	53.5	56.0	56.0
Goodyear	35.7	30.7	10.9
W. R. Grace	39.6	43.8	30.1
Greyhound[a]	48.1	48.1	48.1
Gulf Oil	43.6	48.4	32.8
IBM	38.7	27.6	27.6
International Harvester	45.4	44.0	12.8
ITT	39.6	43.8	30.1
Kraftco	44.3	44.2	44.2
Lockheed Aircraft	41.8	46.2	46.2
LTV Corp.	38.4	43.1	27.5
Mobil Oil	43.6	48.4	32.8
Monsanto	48.4	43.5	37.7

Table 29 (Continued)

Firm	Retire 1975 (1)	Retire 2010; No Automatic Social Security Increases (2)	Retire 2010; Automatic Social Security Increases (3)
Occidental Petroleum[a]	39.7	39.7	39.7
Phillips Petroleum	43.6	48.4	32.8
RCA	36.6	39.1	39.1
R. J. Reynolds	45.2	47.4	47.4
Rockwell International	36.9	46.6	46.6
Shell Oil	36.9	41.6	26.0
Standard Oil of California	44.5	48.1	39.7
Standard Oil of Indiana	45.9	50.6	35.0
Sun Oil	41.5	46.2	30.6
Tenneco	37.2	41.4	41.4
Texaco	48.0	52.3	38.2
Union Carbide[a]	38.9	38.9	38.9
Union Oil of California	43.6	48.4	32.8
U.S. Steel[a]	51.8	56.2	56.2
United Technologies	38.4	46.4	37.2
Westinghouse Electric	41.4	40.4	40.4
Average	42.1	44.4	35.3

[a] Nonintegrated plan.

SOURCE: Wyatt Company Survey, 1975, exhibits II a, b, and c.

social security benefits. Only 13 percent of the 190 firms in the Bankers' Trust sample were not integrated. Only five firms out of forty-eight large industrial firms with pension plans in the Wyatt survey were not integrated. If benefit payments of integrated plans decline as social security benefits rise, this raises a question of equity. Is it fair to deny private benefits just because public benefits rise? Integration also raises questions concerning the magnitude of the incentive effects of private pensions that remain after adjustments are made for social security.

Eliminating Integration

Firms with integrated benefits may eventually be faced by legislation which eliminates integration. This would affect primarily plans for salaried workers and may, according to Schmitt, affect only 30 percent of all workers covered by private pension plans. Even if integration continues, a second problem is that as social security benefits increase in amount, private pensions would play a declining role in providing retirement income. Private pension benefits could be made superfluous by rising social security benefits. This problem affects both integrated and nonintegrated plans.

Regarding the prospect of changing integration rules, the House Ways and Means Committee report on HR 12855 stated in 1974:

> On the one hand, the objective of the Congress in increasing Social Security benefits might be considered to be frustrated to the extent that individuals with low and moderate incomes have their private retirement benefits reduced as a result of integration procedures. On the other hand, your committee is very much aware that many present plans are fully or partly integrated and that elimination of the integration procedures could substantially increase the cost of financing private plans. Employees, as a whole, might be injured rather than aided if such cost increases resulted in slowing down the rate of growth of private pension plans.[8]

Though the House Ways and Means Committee proposed no immediate action, it did ratify the administrative procedures of the Internal Revenue Service, which prohibited integrated pension plans from using increases in social security benefit levels as a reason for reducing the pension benefits of retired employees or of employees separated prior to retirement but already vested. The committee also tried to freeze integration at 1974 levels until 1976, but was unsuccessful in this attempt. Nonetheless, in the Congress the issue of integration is still important.

The view of the House Ways and Means Committee is that if integration were ended by prohibitive legislation, firms would change pension benefit formulas by simply removing the offset or setting an excess breakpoint of zero. This is most unlikely. Rather, firms would tend to rewrite their pension arrangements so that the total pension funds paid out would remain roughly unchanged. If firms did not rewrite, it would imply that they want to pay more in pension benefits; but if they want to do this, they could eliminate the integration procedure now or change other components of their formulas. Accordingly, elimination of integration need not actually raise pension costs over the long run.

---

[8] Ibid., p. 173.

If integration were eliminated and if firms maintained the previous levels of their pension benefits by altering their benefit formulas, employees would not gain. If, however, gain to employees is the objective of Congress, the legislation may also prohibit change in the pension formulas, thus ensuring growth in private pension costs. Given existing integration formulas, the amount of the increase in private benefits would be approximately half the amount of the social security benefit that retired employees would receive from these firms. This could be very costly.

Even if firms could adjust their pension contributions and benefits downward so that aggregate pension costs remained unchanged after integration was legislatively eliminated, there would be a distributional problem. Table 30 shows replacement ratios under different pension plans for various salary assumptions. Under Plan I, an integrated plan, the spread in total replacement ratios—social security and private plans—between an employee with a low starting salary and low-income growth and an employee with high-income growth is 49 percentage points. Under a nonintegrated plan, say, Plan II or Plan III, the spread is 75 and 74 percentage points, respectively. This type of imbalance could have some serious consequences for employee relations. The point of raising this issue, however, is to show that by eliminating integration, some major changes (here a distributional one) may come about in private plans as a consequence of the fixed wage base in the social security benefit computation.

The Size of Social Security Pensions

A second and considerably broader problem is raised by the emergence of social security as a fairly complete pension program rather than as a social insurance scheme providing minimum support. This development may undermine the efficacy of the private pension plan and lead to a reduced role for private pensions.

Between 1950 and 1972, social security benefits have been increased on ten occasions. Currently, they stand at very high levels relative to preretirement income, and there are good prospects for their continued growth. The history of the social security system offers little solace to those who would prefer reductions or constancy in real benefits. The Social Security Amendments of 1977 represented some willingness to limit future benefit increases, but there is no guarantee that these will not be rescinded.

Table 31 shows social security benefits as a percentage of their salary in the year before retirement for male workers in five different salary categories, retiring from 1952 to 1976 at age sixty-five. For each

TABLE 30

COMBINED RETIREMENT INCOME BENEFITS FROM SOCIAL SECURITY AND PRIVATE PENSION PLANS, INTEGRATED AND NONINTEGRATED PLANS

(percent)

Annual Salary at Entry[a] (dollars)	Rate of Increase in Annual Pay (1)	Final Pay as Percentage of Final Social Security Wage Base (2)	Income from Private Pension plus Social Security Primary Insurance Amount as Percentage of Salary at Age 64			
			Social security only (3)	Social security plus plan I[b] (4)	Social security plus plan II[c] (5)	Social security plus plan III[d] (6)
10,000	4	45	78	90	119	105
10,000	5	60	62	80	103	89
10,000	7	106	40	65	80	66
18,000	5	108	42	67	83	69
18,000	7	190	24	54	63	50
30,000	5	180	25	57	66	52
30,000	7	317	14	48	54	41
30,000	10	727	6	41	44	31

a Thirty years of service at retirement; social security wage base in year of retirement is $72,000.

b Plan I: (1.5 percent of final five-year average pay minus 1.25 percent of social security primary insurance amount) × (years of service).

c Plan II: (1.5 percent of final five-year average pay) × (years of service).

d Plan III: (1 percent of final five-year average pay) × (years of service).

NOTE: The following assumptions are made: entry is at age thirty-five; the consumer price index (CPI) increases at 4 percent a year; and the social security wage base increases at 5 percent a year.

SOURCE: Comment by Edwin F. Boynton, in Colin D. Campbell, ed., *Financing Social Security* (Washington, D.C.: American Enterprise Institute, 1979), pp. 298–299.

TABLE 31

SOCIAL SECURITY BENEFITS AS A PERCENTAGE OF EARNINGS IN YEAR
BEFORE RETIREMENT FOR SINGLE MALE WORKERS AT FIVE
DIFFERENT WAGE LEVELS AT AGE SIXTY-FIVE, 1952–1976

(selected years)

Retirement Date	Minimum Wage	Retail Trade	Service Industry	Manu- facturing	Construction Industry
1952	38	30	29	22	19
1955	44	39	36	32	26
1960	41	37	35	31	25
1965	38	36	32	29	23
1970	43	40	34	32	24
1971	46	43	36	35	25
1972	45	42	34	34	23
1973	53	48	39	38	27
1974	51	47	38	37	26
1975	55	49	40	39	29
1976	58	51	41	40	31

SOURCE: Alicia Munnell, *The Future of Social Security* (Washington, D.C.: Brookings Institution, 1977), p. 64.

category of worker, social security benefits have risen relative to final salary. Since productivity gains in each category resulted in noninflationary salary increases, constant real dollar social security benefits would have resulted in declining replacement ratios. Yet, social security benefits not only kept up with productivity and inflation, they also rose relative to final salary. This trend may not continue, but it is the current level that matters.

Table 32 shows replacement ratios for three income levels for men retiring at age sixty-two and sixty-five on January 1, 1976. Although all ratios are large, low- and medium-income workers do comparatively better than high-income workers, who probably had greater capacity to save privately. Further, Table 32 shows that the differences in replacement ratios for early and normal retirement are not particularly large.

The past and possible increases in social security benefits have important implications for private pension plans. The first and most obvious is that the trend in early retirements is up.[9] Many valuable, skilled employees are probably retiring before the firm would prefer

---

[9] Munnell, *The Future of Social Security*, chap. 4.

TABLE 32

REPLACEMENT RATES ON JANUARY 1, 1976, FOR THREE INCOME LEVELS

Income Level	Male, Aged 62	Male, Aged 62, with Wife	Male, Aged 65	Male, Aged 65, with Wife
Low ($3,439 in 1975)[a]	0.53	0.911	0.663	0.994
Medium ($8,255 in 1975)[b]	0.369	0.635	0.462	0.693
High ($14,100 in 1975)[c]	0.264	0.453	0.330	0.495

[a] Wages prior to 1975 followed minimum wages.

[b] Taxable earnings equal to median taxable earnings in each year.

[c] Maximum social security wage base in each year.

SOURCE: Alicia Munnell, *The Future of Social Security* (Washington, D.C.: Brookings Institution, 1977), p. 26.

them to leave. This has been made possible by the firm's own private pensions and early retirement programs as well as by the dramatic increase in social security benefits, particularly those applicable to early retirement. To reduce this effect, firms could tighten their own requirements, even though this would be difficult to do because of existing contractual agreements.

The Age Discrimination in Employment Act of 1978 bans mandatory retirement before age seventy.[10] In addition, the 1977 amendments to the Social Security Act encourage workers to continue working beyond age sixty-five. The legislation increased the amount that persons aged sixty-five through sixty-nine may earn without losing benefits; it will allow persons aged seventy and seventy-one to receive full benefits without regard to other earnings by 1982; and it increased by 3 percent a year the old-age benefit of a worker who delays retirement past sixty-five.[11] Despite this encouragement to continue working, early retirement is still a very real problem.

A second and more serious result of high and rising social security benefits is the reduction of the efficacy of private pension plans. James Schulz has estimated that to maintain preretirement living standards in retirement, income replacement should be approximately 60 to 65

[10] See Robert M. Macdonald, *Mandatory Retirement and the Law* (Washington, D.C.: American Enterprise Institute, 1978).

[11] See Colin D. Campbell, *The 1977 Amendments to the Social Security Act* (Washington, D.C.: American Enterprise Institute, 1978).

100

percent.[12] For low- and median-income workers, Table 32 shows that social security retirement benefits alone come quite close to providing these income needs. Together with transfers in kind, such as health care benefits, total pecuniary and nonpecuniary income for these workers may be more than necessary. In fact, even for high-income workers, the shortfall between need and social security benefit is not much beyond the lifetime private savings capacity of individuals. Moreover, even for workers who earned considerably more than the social security maximum wage base, the absolute size of the social security benefit, after automatic adjustment for inflation, should exceed the minimum income standards for elderly couples needed to enjoy an intermediate standard of living; this was $6,041 in 1974.[13]

In short, the "need" for a private pension has diminished. Its role of helping retired employees achieve satisfactory living standards during retirement years has, to a measurable degree, been displaced by the social security system's old-age and survivors benefits.

To view this issue from a more theoretical perspective, consider the typical employee's utility for income function. Several researchers have found that there is a diminishing marginal utility for income or, alternatively, a declining marginal rate of substitution of income for leisure.[14] That is, a one-dollar increment to a $500 income is more highly valued than a one-dollar increment to a $1,000 income. Let us now apply this finding to private pensions.

The utility an employee expects to derive from a pension claim (or replacement ratio) of a known size is a function of the magnitude of that claim *and* other income expected to be received over the period during which the pension claim is to be paid off. The utility to the employee of a pension claim of a given size, given the fact of diminishing marginal utility of income, therefore declines as other expected income (for example, income to which the right is certain and guaranteed by government) rises. In the early 1960s when social security replacement was little more than half its current level, a claim to a private replacement ratio of, say, 30 percent provided the worker with more utility than a private pension claim of the same magnitude now.

If one of the prime objectives of private pension plans is to induce employees to remain on the job and to work with reduced monitoring by the firm, the incentive effect of a private pension plan is probably

---

[12] Schulz, *The Economics of Aging*, p. 72.

[13] Greenough and King, *Pension Plans and Public Policy*, p. 212. The reported figure is based on a study prepared by the Bureau of Labor Statistics.

[14] Marshall Blume and Irwin Friend, "The Asset Structure of Individual Portfolios and Some Implications for Utility Functions," *Journal of Finance*, vol. 30 (May 1975), pp. 585–604 and references cited there.

101

positively correlated with the expected utility of the pension benefit. The private replacement ratios that prevailed when social security benefits were comparatively low now provide not only less expected utility to the employee but also less of an incentive to the employee to perform in ways desired by the employer. Social security benefits have thus undermined the private pension system.

For firms to achieve once again the same degree of utility and incentive for employees, private pension benefits (and replacement ratios) must rise. But in light of diminishing marginal utility, they must rise by more than the increase in social security benefits. Pension benefits, in fact, may have to rise by so much that the benefits to the firm fall far short of the costs. Alternatively, firms may simply accept the reduction in the incentive effect of their private pension plans and decide either that the plan should be continued on the ground that the value still matches or exceeds the costs, or that the plan should be abandoned.

When firms initially started their pension plans, the combination of replacement ratios, vesting provisions, and other features were optimal or very nearly so for the particular situation. But the rise in real social security benefits has been greater than firms anticipated, especially within the past several years, and has surely altered the optimal combination of pension plan features, particularly the magnitude of benefits. It would be difficult, however, to make the case that higher real benefits would be advantageous to *both* employers and employees. If they were, employers would already have offered higher benefits. Accordingly, benefits are not very likely to rise enough to offset the detrimental effect of higher social security benefits on the utility of private pension plans. What is more, the most rapid rises in real social security benefits have occurred within the last several years. A reasonable conjecture is that firms have not yet had time to make the necessary adjustments to their private plans. When they do, the plans will become less generous. From the point of view of the firm, if private pensions are curtailed, new ways of motivating workers must be sought. But if there were ways to do this that were less costly per unit of incentive than private pensions, they would already have been used.

Recent empirical work by Alicia Munnell supports the broad conclusion that social security is displacing private pensions, though her work was not explicitly designed to shed light on my particular form of the hypothesis.[15] She finds that the expected level of social

---

[15] Alicia Munnell, "The Future of the U.S. Pension System" in Colin D. Campbell, ed., *Financing Social Security* (Washington, D.C.: American Enterprise Institute, 1979).

security benefits has a depressing effect on total private retirement saving, including pension saving. Moreover, she finds that annual social security taxes reduce annual private savings nearly dollar for dollar.

Two Broad Problems with Social Security

In recent years much has been written about the enormous deficit in the social security program that looms ahead.[16] This expected deficit has important implications for the business firm. The actuaries of the social security system have estimated that the deficit may approximate 0.90 percent of taxable payroll in the years 1977–2000, 3.58 percent of taxable payroll in the years 2002–2026, and 4.63 percent of taxable payroll in the years 2027–2051.[17]

The Social Security Administration does not have a good forecasting record and may be seriously understating the size of this large future deficit. For example, estimates for 1971 made in 1967 underestimated outgo of the system by 46.9 percent, underestimated income by 10.4 percent, and overestimated the balance in the social security trust fund by 25.9 percent.[18]

To cover the deficit, social security tax rates must be raised. In 1978 the payroll tax rate was 12.1 percent on the employer and employee combined on earnings up to $17,300. The 1977 amendments to the Social Security Act raise the combined tax rate on employees and employers in several steps to 15.3 percent in 1990, and the taxable wage base to $29,700 in 1981. But this sharp increase in payroll taxes, though seemingly enormous, is not sufficient to cover the long-run deficits in the social security system estimated for the next century.

For the most part, past increases in social security taxes and wage bases have been announced far enough in advance so that firms could make appropriate adjustments in their pay policies and in their private pension plans. Therefore, in the long run at least, the incidence of the social security tax burden fell primarily on the firm's employees rather than its shareholders or its customers.[19] But if the social security deficit

---

[16] See, for example, Munnell, *The Future of Social Security*, and Van Gorkom, *Social Security—The Long Term Deficit*, for illustrative estimates of deficits and prescriptions for their cure.

[17] A. Haeworth Robertson, *Social Security: Prospects for Change* (Washington, D.C.: M. Mercer, Inc., 1978), p. 12.

[18] F. J. Crowley, "Financing the Social Security System—Then and Now," in Subcommittee on Fiscal Policy of the Joint Economic Committee, 93rd Congress, 2nd session, *Issues in Financing Retirement Income*, Studies in Public Welfare, Paper no. 18 (Washington, D.C., 1974), appendix II, p. 101.

[19] See Brittain, "The Incidence of Social Security Payroll Taxes."

is as large or larger than forecast and if in order to finance that deficit tax rates, the wage base, or both rise with very little warning, a greater portion of the burden will fall temporarily on shareholders and consumers.

Unanticipated increases in social security taxes would probably adversely affect shareholders in industries that face intensive competition from foreign firms not subject to similar tax changes. Also, if firms have some market power because of downward sloping demand curves for their products, they may shift part of the tax to consumers. Among such firms, those that are more labor intensive will have to raise prices more than those that are less labor intensive. This would alter relative prices among different products. Such changes add to the general uncertainty of business decision making and may result in rather substantial welfare costs.

In response to this greater uncertainty, firms might alter their debt-equity financing mix. The higher the degree of uncertainty, the fewer fixed contractual financial obligations firms may want to have. Private pension plans are themselves an important type of fixed financial obligation which firms may wish to reduce because of increased uncertainty. This is another way in which social security tax increases could make existing private pension plans less attractive.

A second broad issue is the effect of social security on private saving. Recent studies by Feldstein and Munnell[20] have concluded that prospective social security benefits reduce net incentives to save, though the magnitudes implied by each study differ. Private pension plans also reduce incentives for individual saving as well.[21] As institutionalized savings (prospective social security benefits and private pension benefits) grow, personal savings decline.

Unlike other sources of retirement income, which represent claims against real assets, social security is backed by claims against future tax revenues. One might expect that social security would induce higher private saving to offset future tax obligations.[22] But this does not appear to be the situation. As social security benefits rise relative to final wages, the benefits of integrated private pension plans fall relative to final wages. As the contractual benefits of private plans fall, the amount of pension fund assets that must be accumulated is

---

[20] See, for example, Munnell, *The Future of Social Security,* chap. 6; and Martin S. Feldstein, "Social Security, Induced Retirement, and Aggregate Capital Formation," *Journal of Political Economy,* vol. 82 (September-October 1974), pp. 902–926.

[21] Munnell, "Private Pensions and Saving: New Evidence."

[22] Robert J. Barro, "Are Government Bonds Net Wealth?" *Journal of Political Economy,* vol. 82 (September-October 1974), pp. 1095–1117.

smaller. Integration, therefore, may lead to less private capital formation.

Rising social security benefits may reduce personal saving as well as aggregate pension plan saving. This would have deleterious consequences for capital formation. The decline in private saving, hence the decline in the demand for financial claims on real assets, may cause the cost of capital to firms to rise and investment activity and economic growth to decline. This could create a serious problem for the social security system, for without real growth the social security benefits that have already been promised will be more difficult to deliver.

7

Looking Ahead

Both ERISA and rising social security benefits will probably reduce private pension fund coverage. The concerns of writers such as Paul Harbrecht and Peter Drucker about the social and economic consequences of continued expansion of the corporate pension system may never be realized.

Writing in the late 1950s, Harbrecht noted:

> The pension trusts are becoming new centers of power in our society. . . . This function (which they perform) is to distribute among the generality of the people the wealth which the corporations are creating. . . . As gross inequality of income tends to disappear, the wealth of corporations could conceivably be parcelled out through greater diffusion of share ownership in the corporations, but this method has not found favor since it involves a risk which the person of small means is unprepared to take. But . . . the pension trusts . . . stand ready to take the capital produced by individuals for reinvestment in the capitalistic system . . . [they] are now rapidly socializing the wealth in the great domains of capitalism, the corporations.[1]

More recently, Peter Drucker has pointed out that pension funds own at least 25 percent of American business equity, enough for control, and that this is akin to socialism. He concluded:

> Pension fund socialism is in the process of creating a genuine new "interest group" . . . a group with clearly defined self-interests. . . . There are three major issues on which the new interest group is held together by common opposition. These issues are, first, the interests of the "welfare society" of the

---

[1] Harbrecht, *Pension Funds and Economic Power*, pp. 280–281.

retirement and pension system against the "welfare state"; second, the interest in productivity to redress its own inequality versus those egalitarian demands that threaten productivity; and, third, the interest in a stable currency as one of priority, if not the first priority, of economic policy. . . . This new interest group has its own representative institution: the pension fund.[2]

Since the early 1950s, corporate pension plans have not become more liberal in terms of the ratio of retirement benefits to final salaries. They have, however, adopted notably more liberal terms for vesting and eligibility. Whether or not these changes are legislatively mandated, it is unlikely that pension plans will continue this trend without losing their true character.

Corporate pension plans are not really corporate philanthropy, nor are they merely deferred wages. Rather they comprise both a deferred wage component and, more important, an incentive component. The incentive component is enforced, in a sense, by vesting and eligibility provisions. As these provisions become more liberal, the value to the firm of the incentive component shrinks. As the benefits to the firm decline, pensions ultimately become no more than deferred wages. The principal advantage of this type of pension plan is the tax deferral on employees' earnings. Recent legislation, however, provides other ways in which this tax deferral privilege may be obtained. If pensions do ultimately become merely deferred wages, there will be less reason for firms to incur the expense of setting up and administering pension plans. The funds that firms set aside in pension plans could instead be given to employees who, in turn, may either deposit them in individual retirement accounts if they so desire or spend them.

ERISA constrains the way firms contract and administer pension plans. For a substantial number of firms, ERISA will raise the cost of pension plans.[3] The amount of the total increase in cost, however, cannot be actuarially determined because the cost consists primarily of reductions in the incentive effects of vesting and participation requirements and inefficiencies resulting from mandating changes in the customary financing arrangements of firms. The only benefit

---

[2] Drucker, *The Unseen Revolution*, pp. 200–202.

[3] See previous chapters and Randall D. Weiss, "Private Pensions: The Impact of ERISA on the Growth of Retirement Funds," in *Funding Pensions: Issues and Implications for Financial Markets* (Boston: Federal Reserve Bank of Boston, 1976), pp. 137–151. Weiss argues that the cost will be small; my argument is that the actuarial costs of the changes mandated by ERISA understate the true costs, and that in any event 3 to 5 percent, when translated to dollars, is a substantial sum.

ERISA yields to firms is that it reduces the uncertainty on the part of workers as to how much of the promised pension benefit they will get. For employees, ERISA makes pension claims safer and more likely to be achieved, but probably at the sacrifice of expected benefits. ERISA will reduce incentives for firms to offer pensions and encourage them to reduce benefit ratios.

The social security system, too, has the effect of discouraging corporate pension plans. Ture argues that workers may have a target for the ratio of retirement to preretirement income.[4] If this is so, rising social security benefit levels will reduce employees' demands for private pensions. While this argument leads to the correct conclusion, it is probably incomplete. Rising social security benefits reduce the incentive effects of corporate pensions (coming as they do on top of social security) because individuals have declining marginal utility for income and wealth. As the incentive effects on employees decline, the firm's incentive to offer private pensions also declines. Moreover, rising social security benefits will result in a reduction in the replacement ratios of private pension plans that are integrated with social security. For many firms, the cash costs of their pension plans—when added to the firm's contributions to the rising level of social security benefits—may be greater than the perceived advantages of offering private plans. There seems to be a type of Gresham's Law at work: bad retirement income programs are driving out the good.[5]

The tax deferral advantages of private pensions have also been eroded. Employees not covered by private plans can now shield some of their income from the tax man through the use of individual retirement accounts. Moreover, recent legislation allows employed spouses to establish IRAs for their unemployed mates, even if the working family member is covered by a pension plan. While IRAs make the tax treatment of pension-covered and uncovered employees more comfortable, they will surely reduce the demand for private pension plans.

Recent work by Munnell underscores the notion that as the percentage of workers covered by private pension plans shrinks, the political support for private plans will also erode. Munnell writes: "With the role of private pensions narrowed . . . the favorable tax provisions [of private pensions], which accrue primarily to workers

---

[4] Ture, *The Future of Private Pension Plans*, chap. 3.

[5] The term "bad" seems well suited to the social security system. The evidence on the program strongly suggests that its pay-as-you-go nature discourages capital formation. Private pension plans, because they are in large part funded, have not had the same deleterious influence on capital formation; they do provide some incentives for employees to avoid shirking and increase productivity, and are, thus, more helpful to our nation's economic system.

with above-average earnings, may receive renewed scrutiny."[6] The revenue loss to the U.S. Treasury was estimated at $5 billion in fiscal 1974 and rose to $6.5 billion in fiscal 1977.[7] Because pension expenditures support primarily upper-income individuals, continued political support for the favorable tax provisions may erode as smaller proportions of lower-paid workers gain anything at all from private pensions.

The thrust, intended or not, of ERISA and the expansion of the social security system means that ultimately a greater portion of the retirement needs of older Americans will be financed from public sources. Moreover, this trend will tend to reduce the value of a now widely used tool in personnel management. Employment contracts will either have to offer things not now included or employers will have to settle for perhaps less control over employees through incentives.

On the other hand, the prevailing private pension system is spotty in coverage, offers uncertain benefits, and is discriminatory because of social security integration. Some would argue that the demise of the private pension system is welcome. However, the principal argument against governmental policies that undermine the private pension system is that employees should themselves be able to decide whether the pension contract they have is satisfactory. Given the range of employment choices, no employee is compelled to accept an employment contract, including pension arrangements, which is unsatisfactory. If private pension plans get shoved aside because of restrictive legislation or increasingly generous social security benefits, the choices open to employees will diminish. This situation can never be viewed as desirable.

A final note concerns effects in the financial market. ERISA rearranges priorities among suppliers of debt capital; through its funding requirements, it also affects the potential benefits to shareholders. Once again, the government has transformed the nature of property rights. This sort of behavior cannot serve as an incentive to capital formation and is of questionable value to the nation in the long run.

---

[6] Alicia H. Munnell, "The Future of the U.S. Pension System," in Colin Campbell, ed., *Financing Social Security* (Washington, D.C.: American Enterprise Institute, 1979), p. 262.

[7] U.S. Senate, Committee on the Budget, *Tax Expenditures: Compendium of Background Material on Individual Provisions* (Washington, D.C., 1976), pp. 114–116.